MONOLITHIC JINAS

Frontispiece

CAVE 32 (J 10-7) Homage to Bāhubali (Gomaṭa)
C. A. D. 810-880.

MONOLITHIC JINAS

[*The Iconography of the Jain Temples of Ellora*]

JOSÉ PEREIRA

MOTILAL BANARSIDASS
Delhi :: Varanasi :: Patna

First Edition : Delhi, 1977

ISBN: 978-81-2082-397-6

Also available at:

MOTILAL BANARSIDASS
41 U.A. Bungalow Road, Jawahar Nagar, Delhi 110 007
8 Mahalaxmi Chamber, Warden Road, Mumbai 400 026
120 Royapettah High Road, Mylapore, Chennai 600 004
Sanas Plaza, Subhash Nagar, Pune 411 002
16 St. Mark's Road, Bangalore 560 001
8 Camac Street, Calcutta 700 017
Ashok Rajpath, Patna 800 004
Chowk, Varanasi 221 0011

PRINTED IN INDIA

BY JAINENDRA PRAKASH JAIN AT SHRI JAINENDRA PRESS,
A-45 NARAINA, PHASE I, NEW DELHI 110 028
AND PUBLISHED BY NARENDRA PRAKASH JAIN FOR
MOTILAL BANARSIDASS PUBLISHERS PRIVATE LIMITED,
BUNGALOW ROAD, DELHI 110 007

रायमूंद मज्या भावाच्या
आनी ति-कार्मेलीनाच्या
पवित्र आनी गोड उगडासाक
हें पुस्तक भेटयतां

To the memory
of my brother
Raimundo (1928-1947)
and of
Tia Carmelina (1895-1969)
Lux aeterna
luceat eis domine

PREFACE

यद्वेदाध्ययनं तथोपनिषदां सांख्यस्य योगस्य च
ज्ञानं तत्कथनेन किं नहि ततः कश्चिद्गुणो नाटके ।
यत्प्रौढित्वमुदारता च वचसां यच्चार्थतो गौरवं
तच्चेदस्ति ततस्तदेव गमकं पाण्डित्यवैदग्ध्ययोः ॥

Bhavabhūti, *Mālatīmādhavam*, I. 7

> If one has studied the Vedas, the Upaniṣads, the Sāṅkhya and the Yoga—what is the use of talking about it? They serve no purpose in writing drama. Dignity, felicity of expression and depth of meaning—if one has these, they alone prove scholarship and genius!

Indian art tradition has few equals in the world, yet its influence on that most receptive of modern art movements, the schools of the modern West, is minimal, quite out of proportion to Indian art's intrinsic excellence as compared, for instance, with that of primitive Africa and modern Japan. One reason for this is the extreme complicatedness of Indian cultural modes, the appreciation of which demands the mastery of much technical detail—such as for example, of iconography in sculpture, of the *karaṇas* in the dance, of the subtleties of *rāga* modulation in music and of the complexity of rhythm, grammar, vocabulary and allusion in *kāvya*.[1]

1. "Le *kāvya* a créé une langage nouveau, largement original. S'il fallait résumer en une formule ses acquisitions, on verrait qu'elles consistent en un équilibre entre des forces opposées, condensation et dilatation, monotonie et variété, atténuation et rénforcement. ... Il y a eu la un mode d'expression qui, dans les conditions generales, de la pensée indienne, a été aussi legitime, disons franchement, aussi *naturel* que tout autre, même s'il peut nous sembler par trop déniée de facilité (mais qu'est-ce qui est facile dans l'Inde ?)......concédons qu'il existent dans les grands oeuvres de l'Inde une harmonie profonde, puissante, entre l'expression et la chose exprimée: c'est peut-être ce qui définit le mieux l'apport du génie indien sur le plan de la création artistique." Louis Renou, "Sur la structure du kavya", *Journal Asiatique* tome 247 (1959), sec. 47, pp. 60-61.

However, what is difficult and recondite can be made doubly so by pedantry, that parade of irrelevant learning, "the too frequent or unseasonable obtruding our own knowledge in common discourse, and placing too great a value upon it".[1] Furthermore, India, as the sanctuary of one great body of religions, the Indic, has for long been condemned to offer the consolations of religion to those of the West who have been unable to find assurance in the tenets of that other great body of religions, the Hebraic, and that on conditions imposed by the Westerners themselves. A modern symptom of this state of affairs is theosophy, whose exegesis of Indian religious terms has more often than not perverted their meaning, and some of whose adepts have worn to rags the platitude of the "spiritual" superiority of India's culture to that of the "materialistic" West.

Consequently, when an awareness of Indian art began to dawn in Europe, there were two choices open to those to whom destiny had accorded the privilege of interpreting that art's ideas—to facilitate the appreciation of the core of its aesthetic greatness by making the skin and pulp light and digestible, or by converting its technical and symbolistic jargon into an absolute. Pedantry and the need to assert Indian superiority prevailed; Indian art appreciation became a kind of theosophy and an apologia for neo-Hinduism : the first world tradition in art—the school of Paris—went its way as if Indian art had never existed.

Since then the study of the latter has not suffered from an excess of critical sensitivity. It has been mainly three things : a discussion of styles; an exegesis of certain Indian religious ideas in the vocabulary of theosophy and of nineteenth-century British idealism; and (for those lacking the aptitude for either of the above exercises) an iconographical puzzle. A select coterie of pedants seems to have resolved that the matter of history of Indian art shall only be that which can be "elaborated by the toil of the dull".[2] Sensitive critics' efforts—

1. Jonathan Swift, *On Conversation*, in Henry Craik (ed.), *Swift, Selections from His Works*, Oxford 1893, vol. II, p. 335.

2. John Ruskin, *Modern Painters*. Vol. IV, part V, Appendix. London Waverley Book ed. 1856, p. 388.

such as those of Kramrisch to examine in Indian art tradition the growth of a distinctive Indian formal complex and its evolution in various regional modes;[1] or of Codrington to base the appreciation of Indian sculpture on a knowledge of its technical development;[2] or of Sivaramamurti to intensify our apperception of the sculptors' vision with the aid of the imagination of the poets[3]—have been submerged in the great theosophical-iconographical current of contemporary Indian art historical thinking.

The mould of the minds of the men carried along in this current is aptly described by William Jones in his epoch-making preface to his Persian grammar, when he speaks of his colleagues in oriental studies. "Most of them", he says, "have confined their study to the minute researches of verbal criticism; like men who discover a precious mine, but instead of searching for the rich ore, or for gems, amuse themselves with collecting smooth pebbles and pieces of crystal. Others mistook reading for learning, which ought to be carefully distinguished by every man of sense; and were satisfied with running over a great number of manuscripts in a superficial manner, without condescending to be stopped by their difficulty, or to

1. Stella Kramrisch, *Indian Sculpture*, Calcutta and London 1933. The ideas on the aesthetic growth of Indian art formulated here were later elaborated by the authoress in her subsequent works, and by her pupil S.K. Saraswati in his *A Survey of Indian Sculpture*, Calcutta 1957.

2. "Worringer's Gothic is the product of the interweaving of scholasticism and mysticism, racially determined. Very much of the same interpretation has been given to mediaeval Indian sculpture...Worringer's German argument concerning Gothic is closely parallelled by various Indian nationalist arguments concerning Indian Art: both come as a kind of belated pre-Raphaelitism, cumbered with much sentiment...

In the face of this complexity, it is better to return to the stones themselves...A knowledge of the abstruse subject of Indian iconography does not contribute materially towards the appreciation of Indian sculpture. A knowledge of its technical development does". K. de B. Codrington, *An Introduction to the Study of Mediaeval Indian Sculpture*, London 1929, pp. 21-23.

3. See C. Sivaramamurti, "Painting and Allied Arts as Revealed in Bāṇa's Works", in *The Journal of Oriental Research*, Madras 1933, pp. 59-68, for an analysis of colour sense in the greatest of Sanskrit prose writers—which shows the awareness of the nuances of colour among the speakers of Sanskrit, and consequently, among the artists of ancient India.

dwell upon their beauty and elegance. The rest have left nothing more behind them than grammars and dictionaries; and though they deserve the praises due to unwearied pains and industry, yet they would, perhaps, have gained a more shining reputation, if they had contributed to beautify and enlighten the vast temple of learning, instead of spending their lives in adorning only its porticos and avenues.

There is nothing which has tended more to bring polite letters into discredit, than the total insensibility of commentators and critics to the beauties of the authors whom they profess to illustrate; a few of them seem to have received the smallest pleasure from the most elegant compositions, unless they found some mistake of a transcriber to be corrected, or some established reading to be changed; some obscure expression to be explained, or some clear passage to be made obscure by their notes.

It is a circumstance equally unfortunate that men of the most refined taste and the brightest parts, are apt to look upon a close application to the study of languages as inconsistent with their spirit and genius: so that the state of letters seems to be divided into two classes, men of learning who have no taste, and men of taste who have no learning."[1] In Cicero's words *doctis eloquentia popularis et disertis defuit*,[2] "the learned lack agreeable eloquence and the eloquent, accurate knowledge".

It seems then that involvement with Indian iconography destroys the awareness of the art hidden behind the iconographers' commonplaces. Iconography, especially an involved one, is for religion only a necessary evil, and directions to image-makers do not make pleasant reading. No Indian iconography is more tedious and repetitive than the Jain : it would therefore appear that a scrutiny of its clīches would infallibly obliterate any delight in the works of art carved to conform to them.

Could it perhaps be a challenge instead ? It cannot be denied that icon-makers' formulae, if not "learned without

1. William Jones, *A Grammar of the Persian Language*, 9th ed. London 1828, pp. ii-iii.

2. Cicero, *Orator*, iii, 13.

sense" are certainly "venerably dull"[1] but it is also true that some of India's greatest sculptors—such as those of Ellora—were not frustrated by them : this is obviously because, when Indian art was a living thing, symbols were not the fetish that iconographers have now made them. How then can the interpreter of this great tradition—while conscious of the importance of symbols in the understanding of icons and aware also that symbols are not the ultimate in art criticism—preserve his sense of proportion and his sensitivity to the aesthetic joy behind the veil of iconographical cliches ? Simply by eschewing pedantry: *by not talking too much about things which cannot be expressed in visual terms*. The five activities of Śiva, for example, are a noble theme for theological disquisition, but cannot be said to be expressed in the figure of an elegant god, smiling somewhat complacently to himself and standing in a dance posture on the back of a slightly bewildered crawling dwarf.[2]

1. "With various readings stored his empty skull,
Learn'd without sense, and venerably dull."
Charles Churchill, *The Rosciad*, I, lines 591-592.

2. Present-day Indian art criticism is burdened with esoteric concepts because most of its adepts are unable to write *art criticism* or because they wish to hide the mediocrity of some of their *objets d'art* within the depths of a spurious profundity—the latter being often employed to exalt the glories of nation or religion. The *reductio ad absurdum* of this attitude is best expressed by D.H. Lawrence, in his contemptuous description of symbolism in Christian art:

"She saw the ruby-coloured glass, with the shadow heaped along the bottom from the snow outside, and the familiar yellow figure of the lamb holding the banner, a little darkened now, but in the murky interior strangely luminous, pregnant.

She had always liked the little red and yellow window. The lamb, looking very silly and self-conscious, was holding up a forepaw, in the cleft of which was dangerously perched a little flag with a red cross...Yet she had always been uneasy about it. She was never sure that this Lamb with a flag did not want to be more than it appeared. So she half mistrusted it, there was a mixture of dislike in her attitude to it...

'And I think that Lamb in Church', she said, 'is the biggest joke in the parish—'

She burst into a 'Pouf' of ridiculing laughter.

'It might be, to those that see nothing in it', he said. 'You know, it's the symbol of Christ, of His innocence and sacrifice'.

A knowledge of the Vedas, the Upaniṣads, the Sāṅkhya and the Yoga is indeed of little help in the study of art.

II

سعدیا روز ازل حسن بر افغان دادند
عقل و دانائی و فرهنگ بر ایران دادند
عشوه و ناز و نزاکت همه بر مردم هند
خری و خرصفتی جمله به ترکان دادند

Sa'adi ?[1]

> O Sa'adi, on the first day they gave beauty to the Afghans; intelligence, knowledge and culture to Persia; coquetry, pride of beauty and elegance to the people of India; asininity and dullness to the Turks.

This is a work on an iconography of a particularly dull and sterile sort; unless mastered, it will impair full participation in the sculptors' imaginative excitement which the formulae

> 'Whatever it means, it's a *lamb* !' she said. 'And I like lambs too much to treat them as if they had to mean something. As for the Christmas-tree flag—no—'
>
> And again she poufed with mockery.
>
> 'It's because you don't know anything', he said violently, harshly 'Laugh at what you know, not at what you don't know.'
>
> 'What don't I know?'
>
> 'What things mean.'
>
> 'And what does it mean?'
>
> He was reluctant to answer her. He found it difficult.
>
> '*What* does it mean?' she insisted.
>
> 'It means the triumph of the Resurrection.'
>
> She hesitated, baffled, a fear came upon her. What were these things? Something dark and powerful seemed to extend before her. Was it wonderful after all?
>
> But no—she refused.
>
> 'Whatever it may pretend to mean, what is *is* a silly absurd toy-lamb with a Christmas-tree flag ledged on its paw—and if it wants to mean anything else, it must look different from that."
>
> D. H. Lawrence, *The Rainbow*, ch. 6, Penguin Books 1966, pp. 159-162.

1. My friend Dr Iraj Qadimi, of Teheran, from whom I got the verse, claims that it is a verse of Sa'adi's; however, I have not been able to find it in any of the collections of Sa'adi's works that I have consulted.

could not extinguish. It is possible to suggest in words what this excitement consists in? I believe it is.

For the Persians, who stood between the Turkish, Afghan and Indian worlds and constituted themselves the judges of their peoples, India was the home of elegance. In this they were right; traditional Indian aesthetics invests everything it touches with finesse, even the emotions of terror and disgust;[1] I am not aware that this is found in any other literature. As time passed, the arts of the Hindu sects became satiated with elegance; only Śaivism, with its dark power and virulence, possessed the strength to resist being cloyed by it :

> सततममृतादेवाहाराद्यदापदरोचकं
> तदमृतभुजां भर्ता शम्भुर्विषं बुभुजे विभुः ॥[2]

> The mighty Śiva, the lord of the gods, swallowed poison because he was surfeited with nectar, a food he was accustomed to having every day.

The other sectarian mythologies have subjects of greater drama and voluptuousness than Jainism; elegance for them was no more than a mode of expression; Jainism, lacking themes with a wide emotional range, had elegance not only as

1. Even Bhavabhūti, who describes horrific scenes with such gruesome power in his *Mālatimādhava*, cannot wholly resist the common *kāvya* urge to prettify the macabre with the imagery of cosmetics :

> अन्त्रैः कल्पितमङ्गलप्रतिसराः स्त्रीहस्तरक्तोत्पल-
> व्यक्तोत्तंसभृतः पिनह्य सहसा हृत्पुण्डरीकस्रजः ।
> एताः शोणितपङ्ककुङ्कुमजुषः संभूय कान्तैः पिब-
> न्त्यस्थिस्नेहसुराः कपालचषकैः प्रीताः पिशाचाङ्गनाः ॥
>
> *Mālatīmādhava*, V. 18

"The delighted fiend-wives—with auspicious bracelets of entrails, with prominent red-lotus ear-ornaments formed of women's hands, with lotus garlands of hearts put on hastily, with forehead marks of clotted blood—drink the wine of bone-marrow from skull-cups in the company of their demon lovers."

2. Harṣa, *Naiṣadhacarita*, *Sarga* 19.34. See Martial, *Epigrams*, bk 11,57 : Juppiter ambrosia satur est et nectare vivit nos tamen extra Iavi cruda merumque damus.

a mode, but in a fashion also as subject : and the Ellora Jain temples are without doubt the most exquisite productions at that great site.

The perfect proportion of the figures in the Jain caves are an index to this elegance. In the first great period of Ellora carving, the sculptors were primarily interested in the bust, after chiselling which they seem to have been in a haste to finish the torso and the legs, the latter members being often woodenly modelled and in bad proportion.[1] This fashion culminated in the great bust Maheśamūrti of Elephanta, in which cave, however, the proportions of the full-length figures are perfect. In the next phase of Ellora sculpture, whose masterpiece is the Kailāsa, the figures are well-proportioned, but endowed with more power than grace. But in the Jain caves at Ellora we have any number of beautifully-formed young men (the tīrthaṅkaras) and what I believe is the loveliest woman in Ellora, an Ambikā in a small cave of the Indra Sabhā complex;[2] indeed, her coquetry, pride of beauty and elegance have few equals in Indian art.

III

एको रागिषु राजते प्रियतमादेहार्धहारी हरो
नीरागेषु जिनो विमुक्तललनासङ्गो न यस्मात्परः ।
दुर्वारस्मरबाणपन्नगविषव्यासक्तिमूढो जनः
शेषः कामविडम्बितो हि विषयान् भोक्तुं न मोक्तुं क्षमः ॥

Bhartṛhari, *Śṛṅgāraśatakam*, verse 78

Among the impassioned the only outstanding being is Śiva, who takes away half his wife's body. Among the passionless, it is Jina, who forsook the company of women; no one excels him in that class. But other people, dull with the suffusion of the poison of the serpent—love's irresistible arrow—and tortured by lust, can neither enjoy things or free themselves from them.

1. See, for instance, the great Buddha image in the Vishvakarma cave (cave 10) at Ellora.
2. In the cave which I have numbered J̇ 11.

The emotional peak of elegance is a kind of tranquillity-*śānta*, the *rasa* that in the Śaiva temples dominates the other *rasas*, and in Jain temples absorbs them all. As Veṅkaṭanātha suggests,[1] there is an element of coarseness in every other *rasa* : *śṛṅgāra* tends to be indecent, *vīra* piles up mutual abuse between the contestants, *adbhuta* often portrays the impossible; the *rasas* that remain are rather tasteless : only *śānta* can calm mental tension. In other words, emotional tumult ill accords with passionlessness and peace, but elegance is in full harmony with the latter's spirit : passionlessness finds its highest expression in Jina as passion does in Śiva—and some of the greatest masterpieces of the cults of Jina and Śiva are the rock temples of Ellora.

1. Veṅkaṭanātha, *Saṅkalpasūryodaya*, *prastāvanā*, verse 19.

ACKNOWLEDGMENTS

Visitors to Ellora see the Jain temples only after they have looked at the Buddhist and Brahmanical ones, that is, when exhausted after their mile-long walk, and with their visual memories loaded with powerful images. They can then be hardly expected to have any interest left for the Jain sculptures, and their indifference not seldom turns to revulsion on their being confronted with the wild proliferation of images on the ill-lit cave walls, and which is so oppressive to the wearied sight and brain. To me the task of deciphering the significance of these images appeared formidable, and I should never have undertaken it but for the help given me by K. Padmanabha Rao, then (1964) guide-lecturer at Ellora. Rao, to whom each identification was a momentous discovery, communicated some of his passion to me.

This book was originally intended to form a section of the third part of a comprehensive *Survey of the Temples of Ellora*, of which Prefessor K. de B. Codrington, now Professor Emeritus of Indian Archaeology in the University of London, was to have written the first part (on the Buddhist temples) by himself, and the second (on the Brahmanical ones) with my collaboration. We visited the Jain caves together in 1964, and he made many suggestions which have helped me to write this book. He also read through the first two chapters the following year. For all this I am most grateful. I am also thankful to the Jain Digambara monk Aryanandi of Paithan (whom I met at the Ellora Jain Gurukul in the year of my visit) for clarifying some points of Jain doctrine : to Mr R. J. Shah, Director of the Gurukul, for his helpful attitude, to D. P. Nanda, photographer of the former American Academy of Benares,* for sparing no efforts in taking the photographs, to Mr V. K.

*Now the American Institute of Indian Studies, from whose collection, and with whose kind permission the Photographs used in this book have been published.

Venkatavaradhan, also of the Academy, for managing to find the leisure to type this work carefully, notwithstanding the heavy demands on his time, and finally to Mr. B. Srinivasa Bhat, of National Museum, New Delhi for preparing the Index.

CONTENTS

CHAPTER I

JAINISM AND ITS ART

I JAINISM

1 Prehistory
2 Mahāvīra
3 The Schism
4 The Expansion Westwards
5 The Southern Thrust

II JAIN ART

1 Prologue to Iconography
2 Evolution of Jain Art and Iconographical Forms
  a The Growth of the Icon
  b Rock-cut Friezes
  c Monolithic ensembles
  d Elaboration and Innovation

I JAINISM*

1 *Prehistory*

For his followers, the historical founder of Jainism is only the last of a long series of enlightened teachers. The most important of them for the sculptors are Ṛṣabha or Ādinātha, and Pārśvanātha; to a certain extent Śāntinātha; and perhaps Supārśva and Nemīnātha too.[1] Historians of Jainism consider the first twenty-two mythical. They are agreed on Mahāvīra's historicity and seem also to accept Pārśvanātha's. The latter teacher, for the artists and poets perhaps the most popular of all tīrthaṅkaras, is supposed to have been born at Benares 350 years before Mahāvīra, and to have died at the age of hundred. Among the followers of his doctrine were the parents of Mahāvīra himself.

2 *Mahāvīra*

The last of the tīrthaṅkaras, according to many accounts, was born of the brāhmin Ṛṣabhadatta and his wife Devanandā, inhabitants of the city of Vaiśāli. The gods trans-

*Unless otherwise mentioned, the contents of this chapter are taken from ch. 12, paragraphs 2387-2494, pp. 609-664 of Louis Renou & Jean Filliozat's *L'Inde classique : Manuel des études indiennes*, Paris : Imprimerie Nationale 1953, vol. 2; of the paragraphs referred to, 2387-2454 are Louis Renou's, 2455-2492 Olivier Lacombe's, and 2493-2494 Jean Filliozat's.

1. The following are the names of the 24 *tīrthaṅkaras* :

1.	Ṛṣabha or Ādinātha	13.	Vimala
2.	Ajita	14.	Ananta or Anantajit
3.	Sambhava	15.	Dharma
4.	Abhinandana	16.	Śāntinātha
5.	Sumati	17.	Kunthunātha
6.	Padmaprabha	18.	Aranātha
7.	Supārśva	19.	Mallinātha
8.	Candraprabha	20.	Munisuvrata
9.	Puṣpadanta	21.	Nami
10.	Śītala	22.	Nemīnātha or Ariṣṭanemi
11.	Śreyāṁsa	23.	Pārśvanātha
12.	Vasupūjya	24.	Mahāvīra

ferred Devanandā's embryo to the womb of a Magadhan princess Triśalā, who dreamt fourteen marvellous dreams before this happened. She was married to chief of the Nāta clan; hence Mahāvīra was often called Nātaputta. In many texts, however, the transfer of the embryo episode is omitted.

The child was brought up with princely care, and learnt all the arts and sciences. When he came of age he married a noblewoman called Yaśodā, and had a daughter by her. When he was 28, however, he lost his parents and decided to renounce the world. With his elder brother's permission he left his family, distributed all his riches to the poor, put on an ascetic's robe, and went to live in a park near his native city. Thirteen months later, he threw away his clothes, became a wandering beggar and punished himself with harsh austerities. Except during the rains, he did not stay in any fixed place. He was mocked and ill-treated, and bore these and other privations for twelve years. In the thirteenth year he entered into a long period of mortification, at the end of which he meditated concentratedly under a teak tree for a solid two-and-a-half days. Then he saw light and became the all-knowing Arhat, free from the bonds of transmigration. To those who accepted his teaching he was the Jina, or "conqueror"—whence his followers are called Jains. To the gods, he became "the great hero" or Mahāvīra.

The remaining 30 years of his life were spent in constant wandering and in frequent preaching. He covered only a limited area of north-eastern India in his travels, staying for the rains chiefly at Vaiśāli, Śrāvasti and Rājagṛha. He died at Pava, near modern Patna, at the age of 72, reciting sacred texts. The sect which commissioned the Ellora Jain sculptors believes this to have happened in A.D. 78.

3 *The Schism*

Unfortunately for the Jains, Mahāvīra did not commit his sacred texts to writing. Jainism, like other religions, had its focal point of disunity: for Islam it is succession to the Prophet; for Christianity, primacy among the successors of the Apostles. In Jainism it appears to have been principally the transmission of the sacred texts, though, later, nudity was given as the true reason. The memory of the authoritative inspired teaching gradually failed until, says the nudist sect, it was totally lost. The first successors of Mahāvīra *knew* all of it; they were *kevalins*. Then came those who had *heard* all of it, *śrutakevalins*. The last of the latter is supposed to be Bhadrabāhu. His contemporaries only knew some of the inspired sentences; thus an urgent need was felt to collect all of them, and a council was convened in Pāṭaliputra to establish a canon. Unfortunately, the man who could have helped most—Bhadrabāhu—was at that very moment on his way to Nepal, and the emissaries sent to him did not come back with all the texts.

In the meantime, a great famine was scourging northern India, and Bhadrabāhu, back from Nepal, found himself obliged to go south with a large part of the Jain community. Those unwilling to accompany him were allowed to remain under the leadership of Bhadrabāhu's disciple Sthūlabhadra. Bhadrabāhu chose Shravana Belgola in the Karnataka for his "see", thus making it the holiest place of pilgrimage for the nudist sect—under whose inspiration the Ellora Jain caves were carved—and hence turning the "lovely Karnata country" into "the cherished abode of the Jaina religion".[1]

When the famine was over, some of the emigrants went back to Magadha. So far all Jain monks had been totally nude; now some of those who had weathered the famine were found to cover their genitalia with pieces of white cloth. One sect thus came to be called "sky-clad" or nudist (*Digambara*), and the other "white clad" or clothed (*Śvetāmbara*). Nudity or clothing was a concrete symbol of a deeper dissent, and, (as

1. "By its roaring waves and dashing spray proclaiming that it had mountains and pearls was the ocean surrounding Jambudvīpa, in the middle of which was mount Meru, south of which was the land of merit Bharata-Khanda. Among the many beautiful countries it contained, an abode of the Jina-dharmma, a mine of good discipline, like the dwelling of Padmāsana (Brahma), having acquired great fame, the birth-place of learning and wealth, the home of unequal splendid earnestness—thus distinguished in many ways was the lovely Karṇṇāta country." Sorab Taluk Inscription 261 (A.D. 1408), *Epigraphia Carnatica*, Vol. VIII, Inscriptions of the Shimoga District (part 2), ed. B. Lewis Rice, Bangalore 1904 (Mysore Archaeological Series).

I said) the transmission of scriptures was perhaps the chief point at issue. The Digambaras believe that the texts disappeared, the Śvetāmbaras hold that they are preserved in fragments.

4 *Expansion Westwards*

The main currents of Jainism moved south and west. Bhadrabāhu's journey south was probably motivated by the fact that there was an appreciable Jain community there already. Both sects shifted west, but the more west they went, the more Śvetāmbara their doctrine seemed to become: for while the Mathura and Gupta sculptural corpora are all Digambara, those of Vasantgarh and Akota are Śvetāmbara. This latter sect was sufficiently numerous in the west by the second half of the fifth century to hold a council of its own at Valabhi, under the leadership of Devarddhi. The secondary treatise of the Jain canon was compiled, and the scriptures definitively fixed for the Śvetāmbaras.

Established in Gujarat and Rajasthan, Śvetāmbara Jainism lived through trials and spells of fortune until the tenth century, when the Kalacuris enthusiastically championed its cause. But its moment of triumph was the reign of Kumārapāla (king between 1200 and 1229), patron of Hemacandra—Jainism's most prolific genius, one of the few on whom Sanskrit learning has conferred the title *sarvatantrasvatantra*, "self-sufficient in all fields". The two centuries on either side of this king's reign were some of Jainism's most fortunate ones; during this time some of its loveliest shrines were erected.

5 *The Southern Thrust*

Quite early in its history, Jainism took root in the peninsula—where it excelled Buddhism in popularity—and helped fashion the region's culture into a shape that it afterwards never quite lost. Some of the great classics in Tamil and Kannada are the work of its votaries. For a time the Jains were vigorous in Orissa, supported partly by royal patronage, which they also received from some Andhra princes,[1] and also in parts of present day Maharashtra, from the Śātavāhanas.[2] Some of the monarchs who favoured them were from the Pallava, Cālukya, Rāṣṭrakūṭa, Gāṅga and Hoysala families. While the Jains owe the Rāṣṭrakūṭas the monolithic temples of Ellora,[3] it is the Gāṅgas—those most dedicated of Jain dynasts—who gave them the granite colossus of Shravana Belgola.

The Hoysalas, in the beginning, were also devout Jains, but one of their members was converted to the cult of Viṣṇu by Rāmānuja. Beside Vaiṣṇavism, first Āgamic Śaivism and then Vīraśaivism[4] struck the gentler and less exciting religion blows under which it finally succumbed. The Pallavas became Śaivas, the Rāṣṭrakūṭas were mostly Śaivism prone and the Cālukyas often behaved in an unfriendly manner to Jains. The Pāṇḍyas were openly hostile; the Muslims brutal; and though there was a revival under the empire of Vijayanagar, one could see that by the twelfth century the high noon of South Indian Jainism had passed.

II JAIN ART

Art is more closely linked with the cardinal ideas and significant moments of Jainism than it is with those of some other art-loving religions, such as Christianity and Islam. For instance, after the enlightenment of the tīrthaṅkara, the gods erect a pavilion (*samavasaraṇa*) of sumptuous materials and imposing proportions for his first sermon—a strong contrast to the simple low hill which Christ chose for his Sermon on the Mount. Similarly the mansions of the gods are conceived

1. P.B. Desai, *Jainism in South India and Some Jaina Epigraphs* [Jīvarāja Jaina Granthamālā No. 6], Sholapur : Jaina Saṁskṛti Saṁrakṣaka Saṅgha 1957, ch. II, pp. 3-24.

2. *Ibid.*, p. 101.

3. For a loose Rāṣṭrakūṭa Jain sculpture see the Jain memorial pillar from Danavulapadu, Cuddapah Dist. (10th century A.D.). F.H. Gravely and C. Sivaramamurti, *Illustrations of Indian Sculpture, Mostly Southern*, Madras : Madras Government Museum 1939, pl. XXIV.

4. B.A. Saletore, *Mediaeval Jainism with Special Reference to the Vijayanagara Empire*, Bombay 1938, ch. 7, pp. 279-282.

in architectural terms elaborate enough to make the "many mansions"[1] of Christ's Father's house appear a very weak metaphor when placed alongside, and to make the *houri*-stocked paradise of Mohammed look very rural and primitive indeed.[2]

Still, post-scriptural Islam and Christianity became more deeply committed to art and monumentality than did Jainism: Mahāvīra's religion produced no counterpart to Santa Sophia of Constantinople or to the Masjed-e-Shah of Isfahan. Yet it is fair to say that the paucity of Jain monuments is in no small measure due to the vandalism of the Muslims, one of the activities in which the latter have always been efficient. The resulting litter of fragments is a source of exasperation for a historian desirous of seeing the growth of Jain art steadily and of seeing it whole.

1 *Prologue to Iconography*[3]

Limited as the material is (and thus tempting to the scholar who is on the look out for a terrain both unexplored and seemingly easy to explore), I shall not attempt a careful survey of the known works of art, but only dwell on the growth of iconographic concepts and pause to examine briefly some of the summits of the Jain art achievement. There is perhaps no other tradition of image making, and certainly not in India, which draws so heavily on the idea of the sage in contemplation—and which also perceives so few of this idea's possible nuances.

The hard core of Jain iconography consists of the sage (a) standing, with his arms hanging loose at his sides or (b) sitting cross-legged. Both these must not have the line of the robe (of the Buddhist) or of the sacred thread (of the brahmin). The negative character of this central concept brings out the poverty of Jain iconographical thinking, and I can think of no positive note that can give a specific Jain colouring to the generic idea of a contemplating sage.

1. John 14, 2.
2. *The Quran*, Suras LV and LVI.
3. See V.S. Agrawala's interesting article "Some Iconographic Terms from Jaina Inscriptions", *Jaina Antiquary* V-2 (Sept. 1939), pp. 43-47.

Four layers surround this core; they indicate the value of subsidiary concepts to the main one of the core. The first layer comprises the symbols employed to indicate the sage's individual personality or identity. These are of two kinds: those closely linked with his person, like the long hair on the shoulders of Ṛṣabha, Pārśvanātha's hooded serpent, and Bāhubali's creepers. The second kind consists of objects drawn or carved near the sage (say on the pedestal or throne) like a deer in the case of Śāntinātha and a bull in that of Ṛṣabha. This latter kind is a later development, fixed only after the eleventh century, and not found in the main body of our sculptures.

The contemplating sage with these symbols is common to all Jainism; it is the problem of his clothes that is crucial. While it is true to say that the nude ascetic without robe and ritual paraphernalia is found only in Jain art, he is now not distinctive of Jainism as a whole (as he was once) but only of its nudist sect. This brings us to the second layer of this iconographic organism, the concept of a sage's superhuman servants (*śāsanadevatās*) the *yakṣa* and *yakṣī*, whose presence defines the identity of the tīrthaṅkara even where the symbols are lacking. From a relatively early period we find a *yakṣa* and a *yakṣī* accompanying several tīrthaṅkaras; the male is Sarvānubhūti and the female, Ambikā. But later each tīrthaṅkara could have only a fixed pair, and the traditional one was assigned to Neminātha alone.

The other superhuman beings, less popular among the Jains than the attendant *yakṣas*, are a miscellaneous assortment of gods borrowed or adopted from Hinduism. These constitute our third layer. In our fourth and last layer—that of the episode—nearly all these elements converge in the tīrthaṅkara's first Sermon (*samavasaraṇa*), and in the two most popular episodes of the Ellora Jains: the temptation of Pārśvanātha and the homage to Bāhubali. The Jains did not exercise the wider choice in episodes that their mythology provided them with, as a perusal of Hemacandra's long *kāvya* on the lives of Jain great men will show.

2 *Evolution of Jain Art and Iconographical Forms*

The course of Jain art appears to fall into two clear divisions; the first from the beginnings to around the eleventh century, the second from that century to modern times. The first period saw the evolution of the basic iconographical ideas, which are only weakly distinctive when confronted with those of Buddhism and Hinduism. The second period witnessed both the codification of the iconography and striking innovations in architectural and sculptural forms.[1]

It is more convenient to divide these two periods into the following four phases:

a The Growth of the Icon
b Rock-cut Friezes
c Monolithic Ensembles
d Elaboration and Innovation

The first three constitute our first period and the fourth our second.

a *The Growth of the Icon*

The simple iconography analysed above into a core and four layers did not fully begin to evolve before the Kuṣāṇa period, though some scholars claim to find traces of it even in the Maurya age.[2] The large Lohanipur torso,[3] for example, is put forth as an instance of an image of a Jain ascetic. This claim can be examined on three points (i) its total nudity, (ii) its "Maurya" polish, and (iii) its stylistic characteristics. In the absence of any other symbol or convention, total nudity cannot conclu-

1. See U.P. Shah, "Seven Bronzes from Lilvā-deva (Panch Mahals)", *Bulletin of the Baroda Museum and Picture Gallery*, IX-1, 2 (1952-53), p. 46.

2. *Ibid.*, *Studies in Jaina Art*, Benares : Jaina Cultural Research Society 1955, ch. I, p. 5.

3. For the Lohanipur torso K.P. Jayaswal, "Jaina Image of Maurya Period", *Journal of the Bihar and Orissa Research Society* XXIII (March 1937), pp. 130-132, and A. Banerji-Sastri, "Mauryan Sculptures from Lohanipur, Patna", same journal, XXVI (1940), pp. 120-124. See also Anonymous, "Oldest Jain images Discovered. Old theories on Jain Iconography upset. Dr. K.P. Jayaswal Interviewed". *Jaina Antiquary* III-1 (June 1937), pp. 17-18.

sively prove a torso to be a Jina's; one must be able to see, for instance, if the arms are long and reach down to the knees (a concept fixed by post-Maurya iconography). The fact that the forearms and knees are broken make it impossible for us to judge. The finding of a smaller figure with long arms (probably of later date) alongside the above-mentioned torso strengthens the claim made for it, and also the fact that we know few (if any) erect nude figures of cult as being anything but those of Jain ascetics.

The "Maurya" polish argument is less conclusive, because post-Maurya figures are known to have it, such as the Didarganj *yakṣī*, whose forelock is decidedly a Kuśāṇa convention. The Lohanipur torso shows Graeco-Roman mannerisms in the modelling of the belly. If the torso is thus that of a tīrthaṅkara at all, it is probably not earlier than the Kuṣāṇa period.[1]

The next major pre-Kuṣāṇa work is the frieze in the Manchapuri cave at Orissa.[2] If T.N. Ramachandran's interpretation is correct, it has the earliest Jain ascetic figure known. However, it is precisely this figure that is damaged almost beyond recognition, but enough is left to indicate that it was a seated cross-legged figure. As the cave was Jain, the reverent attitude of the accompanying figures thus goes to indicate that the scene probably represents either homage to a Jain image or a *samavasaraṇa*.

In the Kuṣāṇa and Gupta ages the basic forms of the Jain icon are developed in loose reliefs and images. The Kuṣāṇa corpus is represented mainly in the Kankali Tila figures in the Lucknow Museum,[3] the Kuṣāṇa sculptures of the Mathura Museum,[4] and the Chausa bronzes in the Patna Museum

1. Compare the Lohanipur torso and the Mohenjodaro statuette of a nude man. John Marshall, *Mohenjo-daro and the Indus Civilization*, London : Arthur Probsthain, 1931, Vol I, pl. X, and pp. 45-47.

2. T.N. Ramachandran, "The Mañcapuri Cave", *Indian Historical Quarterly*, 26-2 (June 1951), pp. 103-108.

3. See Vincent A. Smith, *The Jain Stupa and other Antiquities of Mathura*, 1901. Archaeological Survey of India, New Imperial Series Vol. XX. North West Provinces and Oudh. Vol. V. Muttra Antiquities.

4. See J.P. Vogel, *Catalogue of the Archaeological Museum of Mathura*, Allahabad : Govt. Press 1910; and V.S. Agrawala, *Handbook of the*

(believed to belong to the transition to the Gupta age).[1] The Gupta corpus consists, among others, of the sculptures of that age in the Lucknow and Sarnath Museums, of the carvings on the Vaibhara hill, Rajgir,[2] and of some of the bronzes of the Akota hoard.[3]

b *Rock cut-friezes*

The second stage began before the first one was over. The partially crystallized forms of the iconography were transferred to rocks on hills, and spread out in a haphazard fashion, with no thought of a coordination of forms or ideas. Examples are the sculptures on the above-mentioned Vaibhara hill, those on the Udayagiri hill near Sanchi,[4] some of the caves at Udaya-

Sculptures in the Curzon Museum of Archaeology, Muttra, Allahabad 1939; and *ibid.*, *Mathura Museum Catalogue*, part III, Varanası: Prithivi Prakashan 1963, pp. 2-17. See also N.P. Joshi, *Mathura Sculptures* : Mathura: Archaeological Museum 1966, p. 22.

1. U.P. Shah, "Age of Differentiation of Digambara and Śvetāmbara Images and the Earliest known Śvetāmbara Bronzes", *Bulletin of the Prince of Wales Museum of Western India*, no. 1 (1950-1951), Fig. 14 and p. 34. *Ibid.*, *Studies in Jaina Art*, ch. I, p. 13.

2. *Ibid.*, p. 14. See Ramprasad Chanda, "Jaina Remains at Rajgır", *Archaeological Survey of India, Annual Reports* 1925-1926, pp. 125-127.

3. U.P. Shah, *Akota Bronzes* (State Board for Historical Records and Ancient Monuments, Archaeological Series, No. 1), Bombay: Department of Archaeology, Govt. of Bombay 1959. Shah dates the bronze Pārśvanātha of the Prince of Wales Museum to 100 B.C. Khandalawala comments: "With regard to the......Pārśvanātha, it is stated that it cannot be later than 100 B.C., and may be earlier by a century or two. It seems to us it could never be earlier than 200 A.D., having regard to the face and hair. Even that may be too early a date, for it has yet to be decided whether the figure is an early image or is merely archaistic". Review of Shah's *Studies in Jaina Art* in *Lalit Kalā* 3-4 (April 1956-March 1957), p. 126.

4. There are five sculptures in the Jaina cave on Udayagiri hill on a wall face which is broken by a deep passage. To the left of the passage are (1) seated Pārśvanātha, (2) seated Pārśvanātha; to the right are (3) seated Tīrthaṅkara (4) seated Pārśvanātha and (5) seated Pārśvanātha.

The figures are in *padmāsana*, and all have round haloes. In nos. (1), (2) and (4) Pārśvanātha sits on the coils of his snake—which is to my knowledge unusual in Jain sculpture. Wherever the hoods of the snake can be counted, they are seven. All thrones have a centre [no. (2) has only a wheel], most have a wheel and lions, and one [no. (4)] a has wheel, lions, and kneeling devotees. There is a lotus with two rows of petals

giri in Orissa[1] and the friezes of Dhank.[2] This fashion of scattering sculptures over rocks persisted into the next phase, and indeed for long after it was over. Examples in the south are the friezes in the innumerable Jain hills of pilgrimage, such as Kalugumalai[3] and Vallimalai[4]; and in the north, in the massive agglomeration of the rock sculptures of Gwalior hill.[5]

c *Monolithic ensembles*

Here the themes have some ordering according to a plan. Iconography is becoming fixed, though by no means to the extent set out in the later texts. The best ensembles are the cave temples of Badami[6] and Ellora,[7] the basic pattern being the Jain triad—the tīrthaṅkara in the shrine (accompanied by Ambikā and Sarvānubhūti), and Pārśvanātha and Bāhubali

above the throne in the latter sculpture, so is there in no. (3). The umbrella, found in (1), (2), (3) and (4) has only one tier. Tree or leaf like forms appear on each side of the umbrella in (3) and (4).

Pārśvanātha has two attendants, Dharaṇendra and Padmāvatī. Where the hoods have not been destroyed, each has only one.

1. Shah, *Studies in Jaina Art*, ch. I, p. 6, gives the following references for information of the Udayagiri Hill, Orissa—Rajendralal Mitra, *Antiquities of Orissa and Kuraishi*, *List of Ancient Monuments Protected under Act VII of* 1904 *in the Bihar and Orissa Provinces* (1938), pp. 33ff. See also K.N. Tandon, "Rock-cut Cave Architecture of the Jains in Orissa", *Jaina Antiquary* XIX-2 (Dec. 1953), pp. 18-21.

2. H.D. Sankalia, "The Earliest Jain Sculpture in Kāthiāwar "*The Journal of the Royal Asiatic Society of Great Britain and Ireland*, July 1938, pp. 426-430.

3. If there is any work at all on the Jain sculptures of Kalugumalai, it has escaped my attention. P.B. Desai, *op. cit.*, p. 31, footnote 1, knows only of photographs of the sculptures in the Government Epigraphist's Office. There is a photograph of the Pārśvanātha panel in Stella Kramrisch, *The Art of India*, London 1965, pl. 95. Some other loose Jain sculptures in the hills of Tamil Nad are in Tirupparankunram, Alagarmalai, Muttupatti, Kilalavu, Settipodavu and Poygaimalai.

4. T.N. Ramachandran, *Jain Monuments and Places of First Class Importance*, Calcutta : Vira Sasana Sangha 1944, Pl. V-XII.

5. J. Fergusson and J. Burgess, *The Cave Temples of India*, London, 1880, book IV, ch. IV, pp. 509-510. J. Fergusson, *Indian and Eastern Architecture*, London 1910, revised by J. Burgess and R.P. Spiers, vol. II, book V, ch. III, p. 48.

6. Fergusson and Burgess, *op. cit.*, bk IV, ch. II, p. 491.

7. *Ibid.*, bk IV, ch. III, pp. 495-502.

(juxtaposed). Not so well-planned is the arrangement of the Sittanavasal cave temple panels.[1] The ensemble idea does not seem to have caught on, as the custom of haphazard grouping is followed in several later cave temples, such as the Chandor cave near Nasik.[2]

d *Elaboration and Innovation*

In due course, the tīrthaṅkara with his accessories, his identifying emblems, his yakṣa attendants, the whole pantheon of the gods and the favourite episodes of Jain mythology were all rigorously fixed and elaborated. But even more interesting is the extraordinary rise of new forms in sculpture and architecture. It was the southern Digambaras who apparently first conceived the *betta*—monolithic statues of Gommaṭa in compounds on hill tops,[3] of which the first and the greatest example is that at Shravana Belgola (1116-1117), followed afterwards by the colossi of Karkal (1432) and Yenur (1604). Jainism, falling back before the attacks of Vaiṣṇavism and Vīraśaivism, retreated into the wild fastnesses of the Tulu country[4] (where Karkal and Venur are) and into the Konkan.[5] It must have been the inclement climate of these regions that led them to build the barn-like *bastis* like the Hosabasti of Mudabidire (Mudbidri). Later, the Portuguese were forced by Konkani monsoons to give huddled and compact forms to the plans they had brought from expansive Baroque Europe.

The interior of the Hosabasti is rich and elegant, for elegance has for long been a preoccupation with the Jains, particularly in architecture. In the same century in which the Shravana Belgola colossus was carved, the Jains of the north raised some of their finest temples, the Pārśvanātha (c. 1002)

1. T.N. Ramachandran, "Cave Temples and Paintings of Sittanavasal", *Lalit Kalā*, no. 9 (April 1961), pp. 30-54 and figs. 23 (Pārśvanātha) and 24 (*ācārya* of Madura).

2. Henry Cousens, *Mediaeval Temples of the Dakkhan*, Archaeological Survey of India, vol. XLVIII, Imperial Series, Calcutta 1931, pp. 49-50, and pl. LXIV and LXV. The Triṅgalvāḍi cave (c. 14th century) is described on pp. 48-49 and illustrated on pl. LXIV.

3. Fergusson, *op. cit.*, Vol. II, book V, ch. V, pp. 71-72.

4. Saletore, *Mediaeval Jainism*, p. 323.

5. *Ibid.*, *Ancient Karnataka*, I, pp. 404-405.

and Ādinātha (after 1050) of Khajuraho. Further west, the architectural fashions were more than sensitive to the demands of elegance. The love of supple and graceful brackets, slender arches and light domed interiors of the Rajasthani and Gujarati architects possessed the Jain hearts of those territories more than it did the Hindu, and impelled them to chisel out of marble those configurations of white tracery which are the temples of Abu. The first of these, the Vimala Vasahi, was erected not much more than a century after the Indra and Jagannatha Sabhas at Ellora. In all these structures the details are finished with a silversmith's dedication, but in the Abu buildings all sense of the colossal has vanished.

And truly, Jainism does not crave after the colossal, as do Buddhism, Hinduism, Islam and Christianity. One reason for this is its comparative lack of power and drama, for its absolute is not concentrated in one God or in one supreme Reality, but is dispersed over innumerable autonomous selves. Its saints are colourlessly moral, its sinners and malicious beings are not charged with an evil of any excessive potency, and its stories are too uniform to be exciting. Another factor was the lack of continuous patronage by large-landed and religiously committed monarchs and emperors, and the consequent increased dependence for funds on private merchants and businessmen, who lacked the money for scale and thus went in for finish as a substitute.

Yet the Jains could not avoid being affected by the architectural ensemble-mindedness of some of their literary texts, particularly by the hall of discourse for the tīrthaṅkara's first sermon. The Chaumukh temple was the result of this preoccupation. It is a square-formed building with doors on each side, revealing the image within it from four directions. The image is also four-fold (or *caturbimba*)—"auspicious in all directions (*saravatobhadra*)"—representing as it does the tīrthaṅkara delivering his first discourse, along with 3 images of him for the hearers not in front of him. The finest expression of this type is the Ranakpur or Ranpur temple (1440) built in the same Solaṅki style as Abu, and perhaps Jainism's vastest and most complex sacred edifice.[1] Colonnaded courts are also a

1. Fergusson, *ob. cit.*, Vol. II, bk V, ch. III, p. 46.

feature of most Śvetāmbara temples (and also of some *bettas*), where they surround the central temple (or Gommaṭa colossus). Here the ritual requirements of Jainism paradoxically led it to create a type which, with some modifications, subserves the liturgy of an utterly dissimilar faith, Islam. All one has to do is remove the principal shrine and its porch from the centre of the court, wall up the entrances of the cells which surround it—and one is virtually left with a mosque.[1] In this process of adopting pre-existing buildings, Islam—whose sense of a *trionfante universalità*[2] often infuses a colossality into its buildings—capitulated in Jain territory to the sense of the small, delicate and elegant more that it had ever done elsewhere.

The *samavasaraṇa* of the texts is a complex aggregate of buildings, which made the Jains think not only of four-sided temples, but also of the "temple cities" so distinctive of Jainism. Girnar and Palitana (Śatruñjaya) have the best examples of such "cities"; the largest temple in the former dates from the thirteenth century, and the buildings of the latter are chiefly after the fifteenth. Remarkable too are the tall edifices, like the Ṛṣabha or Śrī Allāta tower of Chitor (twelfth century), which later inspired the tower of victory of Rajasthani chieftains (so much more expressive of triumph than Trajan's column). In the south, these pillar-like edifices are paralleled by the temple pillars (*brahmā* and *māna* stambhas) of the Digambara *bastis*, among the most elegant of which is at Guruvayankeri.

From the above stages, we can abstract the precisely iconographical evolution as follows. In the phase of the *Growth of the Icon*, we see the development of the standing and sitting tīrthaṅkara figures. The sitting figure was always the most important for Jainism, and in the sculptures of the Kankali Tila we can almost see it grow iconographically into its final shape. The earliest sculptures have the squatting figure on a

1. *Ibid.* ch. IV, p. 69.

2. "solo Bramante, Michelangelo e Bernini seppero esprimere la trionfante universalità della chiesa Romana". Antonio Muñoz, *S. Pietro in Vaticano*, Rome : Libreria Mantegozza, n.d. [1924?], p. 24.

relatively plain seat, with a one-tiered umbrella over his head; slightly later ones have the accompanying devotees (afterwards to become fly-whisk-holding *yakṣas*), then the lions under the throne, the lotus seat on the throne, the tree behind the ascetic, the flying figures with the garlands, and so on. The standing figure is much less elaborate, and in both standing and sitting figures we see the characteristics of Ṛṣabha and Pārśva already established. In the latter part of this period too, we find the idea of the servants of the tīrthaṅkara brought in, not corresponding, alas, to the neatly specified prescriptions of the iconographers. Several tīrthaṅkaras have the same assistant couple, Sarvānubhūti and Ambikā.

Some of the sculptures of this period show groups of the twenty-four tīrthaṅkaras often with one of them prominent in the centre (*mūlanāyaka*), but the epoch of the *Rock Cut Sculptures* gave better opportunities for this collective appearance of the Jinas—so popular in later sculpture, because of the more extensive surfaces of living rock. The patterned juxtaposition of standing and sitting tīrthaṅkaras was also experimented with. The three-tiered umbrella seems to have become a distinguishing sign of the tīrthaṅkara in this phase.

More than any other, the period of *monolithic ensembles*, was responsible for the episode, chiefly the temptation of Pārśvanātha and the homage to Bāhubali—who himself appears to make his *début* into iconography at this time. The pantheon grows larger and gods and *yakṣas* turn up in larger and larger numbers.

The age of *Elaboration and Innovation* fixed and rigidified iconography. More than ever before, the interminably mushrooming tīrthaṅkaras became items of architectural detail. But the main achievements of this age are non-iconographical: the *betta* and barn-like basti of the South, and the traceried temple, the columnar tower, the *chaumukh* temple and the temple cities of the North.

Chapter II

THE JAIN TEMPLES OF ELLORA

1 Historical Background

2 The Date of the Temples

1 *Historical Background*

The historical setting of the Ellora temples is a drama in two acts, the Rāṣṭrakūṭa and the Yādava, with a long interval, Cālukya rule. The time of the first act is mainly the ninth century, and that of the second, a brief span over the thirteenth : three centuries intervene. During the first period, we find three states—the Rāṣṭrakūṭas, Pratihāras and Pālas—continually at war with one another for the supremacy of an India still largely free of *mleccha* rule. During the second, the Turks devastated considerable areas of it; the remaining land still preserved the character of traditional India, not excluding the interminable monarchical squabbles.

Though he had ancestors who bore the family name, it was really Dantidurga who founded the Rāṣṭrakūṭa dynasty.[1] He was first a vassal of the Cālukya Vikramāditya II, whose feudatory Pulakeśin he helped to rout an Arab invasion in 733. The next expedition he joined was that against Kanchi ten years afterwards (i.e. 743) where he helped defeat the Pallavas and capture their capital city.

Vikramāditya died in 747, and left Dantidurga strong enough to become independent. Intent on extending his dominions, the new king first wiped out the Gurjara kingdom of Nandipuri, then subdued Mālava, and at its capital Ujjayinī performed a sacrifice (*hiraṇyagarbhadāna*) to acquire a divine body. He then annexed eastern Madhya Deśa, and by the middle of the eighth century was lord of most of central and western India. He waged his last great battle against the Deccan Cālukya Kīrtivarman II, and by 753 was master of Maharashtra.

1. A. S. Altekar, *The Rāshṭrakūṭas and their Times, being a Political, Administrative, Religious, Social, Economic and Literary History of the Deccan... during c.* 750 *A. D. to c.* 1000 *A.D.*, Poona: *Poona Oriental Series No.* 36, 1934, and *ibid.*, "The Rāshṭrakūṭa Empire", ch. 1 of *The Age of Imperial Unity* (History and Culture of the Indian People, Vol IV), Bombay : Bharatiya Vidya Bhavan, 2nd ed. 1964, pp. 1-18, especially pp. 6-8. See also Ibid,. "Jainism in the Deccan under the Rashtrakutas", *Jaina Antiquary* XV-1 (Jn. 1949), pp. 24-31. For the origin of the Rāṣṭrakūṭas See Appendix 3.

He did not live long to relax in his glory, for by 758 he was dead. The Cālukyas were defeated but still not crushed. That task was left for his uncle and successor, Kṛṣṇa I, to accomplish. This remarkable emperor overthrew Deccani Cālukya power, scattered the Gāṅgas of Mysore and conquered the Cālukyas of Veṅgi, finding the time and the money to start and (as we shall soon see) finish the excavation of the great Kailasa of Ellora.

Dying around 773, he was succeeded by his eldest son Govinda II. As a youth Govinda had been a valiant fighter, but kingship for him meant little more than the chance to give himself up to unchecked enjoyment. He was pleased to hand over the administration to his ambitious brother Dhruva, who lay low for some time, but seized power as soon as he could. Under him the Rāṣṭrakūṭa banners were carried to the banks of the Kaveri, and in the north his power virtually encompassed the domains of the Pratihāra and Pāla empires, as he had trounced their rulers in his great northern expedition. In 790 the Rāṣṭrakūṭa emperor came back home, and three years later his son Govinda III became king.

This man was perhaps the greatest of the Rāṣṭrakūṭas, as noble as he was brave; he gave back his rebellious elder brother, Sthamba, the latter's viceregal post when he unsuccessfully tried to oust Govinda from his throne. With Sthamba's loyalty won, he turned to the south and intimidated it into submission; then marched north, beat the Pratihāra Nāgabhaṭa II and received the homage of the Pāla emperor. In the meanwhile, the southern Pāṇḍyas, Keralas and Gāṅgas had formed a confederacy against him, but Govinda moved swiftly southwards and scattered them. Still further south, the noise of his victories frightened the ruler of Ceylon into submission. The whole of the subcontinent was now virtually a Rāṣṭrakūṭa realm.

In 814, Govinda III's son Amoghavarṣa succeeded him to the throne; while he was still a minor, the empire suffered from a southern invasion headed by the Veṅgi King Vijayāditya II, but the regent Karkka managed to beat it off. In 830, Amoghavarṣa had grown up and was strong enough to beat aggressors by himself. The Gāṅgas—who, as we know, were fervent Jains were getting more and more powerful. They recaptured many of their dominions and Amoghavarṣa was unable to stop them, except by marrying off his daughter to one of the aggressor princes. And neither were his exploits in the north the spectacular successes of his forefathers.

Yet Amoghavarṣa's reign was on the whole a successful one. He set up the empire's capital in Mānyakheṭa (Malked) and from there enjoyed himself by encouraging the arts of peace (understandably) rather more than those of war. He patronized the mathematician Vīrācārya, the grammarian Sākaṭāyana and the poet and purāṇa-writer Jinasena—author of the *Pārśvābhyudaya*, the *Harivaṁśa* and the *Mahāpurāṇa*. He himself was a poet, and perhaps wrote the first Kannada work on poetics, the *Kavirājamārga*. And he seems almost certainly to have been the one who commissioned the sculptors to carve the Jain cave temples of Ellora.

Most of Amoghavarṣa's reign was troubled by wars and revolts, as was that of his (also Jain-minded) son Kṛṣṇa II, who fought the Cālukyas, Pratihāras and Colas, not always successfully. Indra III, his grandson, again captured Kanauj—the prestige symbol of Indian imperialism—but was not victorious in his fight with the Veṅgīs. His younger son murdered his first-born and successor Amoghavarṣa II, and became Govinda IV. Like another namesake and predecessor, Govinda was debauched too much, so thought his ministers and feudatories, who had him replaced by an uncle of his (crowned as Amoghavarṣa III). But this man was religious and little interested in administration; so he made his son, Kṛṣṇa III, king. This last of the great Rāṣṭrakūṭas triumphed over the Colas and headed a victorious military procession to Rameshvaram where he erected a pillar of victory. In 963, he marched north, as his illustrious predecessors had done.

Eleven years afterwards the Rāṣṭrakūṭa empire had ceased to exist; Kṛṣṇa III's campaigns had taxed it beyond its powers. In 970, the Paramāra revenged his forefathers' defeats by sacking the Rāṣṭrakūṭa capital and in 974 the Cālukya Taila II dealt the empire its *coup-de-grace*. The last Rāṣṭrakūṭa, his thoughts turned to higher things, starved himself to death through the Jain penance *sallekhanā*.

Internecine warfare had long been endemic in India, and the Cālukyas[1] could not avoid being affected by it. More than anything else, the king sought his own glory which—as a poet picturesquely and brutally says—though white, oddly made the faces of the enemies' wives dark.[2] The Cālukyas clashed with the Paramāras in the north, the Hoysalas and Colas in the south; particularly with the latter. In the early years of the eleventh century the Cola Rājarāja the Great ravaged their territory with an army of around nine hundred thousand men. The only Cālukya of interest to us is Someśvara III (reigned from 1126-1138), 'compiler of that famous encyclopedia of mediaeval Indian learning' the *Mānasollāsa*.

Half a century after him, Someśvara's kingdom foundered. A new one was created by Bhillama V, a member of a feudatory dynasty, the Yādavas. It was during the time of Bhillama's grandson—Siṅghaṇa, greatest of the Yādavas—that the second group of the Ellora Jain temples was executed.

Under Yādava rule the Deccan had its first bitter taste of Muslim arms, for Siṅghaṇa skirmished with Iltutmish. But the northern enemy could not be kept away for long, and around forty-seven years after Siṅghaṇa's death, in 1294, Allauddin Khilji pillaged the monolithic Yādava fortress of Devagiri. In 1317, his son, Mubarak, finally reduced it and flayed the last Yādava, Harapāladeva, alive. Twenty eight years afterwards, in 1345, the first Bahmani monarch was crowned in Daulatabad.

The Khiljis behaved with savagery, and both Hindus and Jains suffered. But the Bahmanis were a tolerant dynasty, and inscriptions from Ellora during their period show us that the Hindus at least were worshipping in their temples. There is evidence also that the Jains were using theirs in the thirteenth century; during the latter part of which epoch, however, the

1. D. C. Ganguly, "Later Chālukyas and Kalachuris of Kalyāṇa" *The Struggle for Empire* (History and Culture of the Indian People vol. V), Bombay : Bharatiya Vidya Bhavan, 2nd ed. 1966, ch. VI, pp. 161-183.

2. इन्दुधवलापि कीर्तिर्धवलितभुवनत्रयापि तव नृपते ।
मलिनयति रिपुवधूनां मुखानि यन्नाथ तच्चित्रम् ॥

Somadeva, *Yaśastilaka*, *āśvāsa* 1, v. 159.
Bombay : Nirnaya Sagara Press, 1916, p. 169.

cause of their religion in this part of India was irrevocably lost. The last Jains, of those who had continuously worshipped in the temples from their foundation, probably fled the place on the arrival of the first Muslim armies, and we can be sure that those who remained were not spared.

2 *The Date of the Temples*

The following types of evidence help us to establish the date of the Ellora Jain temples:

1 Epigraphy
2 Palaeography
3 Typology
4 Style
5 The Mechanics of Rock Temple Excavation
6 Historical Background

Epigraphy—that is inscriptions either dated or suggesting a date—aids us little, but its evidence is precious. It tells us that the Kailasa was carved under Kṛṣṇa I, that is around 750-780 (Karka Grant of Suvarṇavarṣa, dated 812-813) and that the great Pārśvanātha relief on the Cāraṇādri hill was executed in 1234-1235 (Appendix 1, Inscription 12, dated). I have shown in Appendix 2 that the Kailasa was finished in one excavation not extending over a great period of time.

Paleography suggests that the undeciphered Kannada reliefs of cave J 26 (Inscriptions 7a, 7b, 7c) may be from about 750 to 850 (according to Fleet) or from 800-850 (according to more recent scholars). The inscription of Śrī Nāgavarma (inscription 8a) is ascribed by Fleet to the 9th or 10th century.

This gives us three dates to work on: that of the Kailasa (c.750-780), that of the cave beneath the Jagannātha Sabhā (9th or 10th century) and the Yādava Pārśvanātha relief (1234-1235). The Kailasa's date is a *terminus a quo* for our third type of evidence, typology, which is a highly complex affair; it is sufficient if we restrict ourselves to its prominent feature, the column, of which, in Ellora, there are three varieties: what we may call the Deccani (āmalaka-padma), the Gangetic (vase-and-foliage) and the Composite (of the two previous orders). The Composite order is totally absent in the Kailasa and the temples that antedate it; it is found in the Lankeshvara, where it seems to have originated and to have spread like a wildfire blaze to many of the Jain caves; the body of the monuments adopting the Composite column is thus posterior to the Kailasa, and may be called the Lankeshvara group.

This group is also compact stylistically. Its temples have in common interior columns with squat and imposing proportions but finished with a fastidious finesse of decorative detail, almost as if the stone were silver (see Illustration 2); they also have a pattern-book repetitiveness of motifs in the ornamentation. It appears as if the Lankeshvara was an audacious breakthrough and that more carefully planned Jain caves were refined developments. Thus, for example, the light in the Lankeshvara enters from a side of the temple, while the Jain caves are so carved that it comes in from the front. The details, more sketchy in the Lankeshvara, are exquisitely finished in the Jain caves, especially in J 20, the most elegant temple in all Ellora. Equally, the Chhota Kailasa architect seems to have been working with an already excavated Kailasa as a model.

The homogeneity of the style leads one to postulate that the temples of the Lankeshvara group are contemporary, or not far removed in date. This supposition is reinforced by a study of the mechanics of cave excavation and of the temples' historical background. When a temple was decided on, a spot was chosen on the hillside. An imaginary line was generally drawn at the lowest level of the slope, from which spot the cutting of the rock proceeded inwards, until the outer crust of the relatively more brittle, cracked and earth-incrusted rock was cut away and a fine hard surface arrived at. The cutters then went on to bore into the rock on the three steep sides of the "trough". When a cave temple was planned, what the excavators were chiefly working towards was the side of the rock opposite the imaginary line, and not those sides adjacent to the lines on its right and left: the rock of the latter, being nearer the surface, was not as good. When the cutters had a free-standing temple in mind, they worked round a lump of rock and then turned the isolated monolith over to the sculptors.

The Jains seem to have gone in chiefly for upper floor caves, as one can see in the Indra and Jagannātha Sabhās; both are top floor temples and the most imposing of the Jain group. Some other caves are ordered in relation to them as complementary to main structures, but no end cave is ever related to a side one as a subsidiary to a principal. The lower floor caves were not given much attention: the one underneath the Indra Sabhā is unfinished and less imposing and the ones beneath the Jagannātha Sabhā are far smaller than the temple above.

Thus, while it is possible that the side caves may have been begun before the main one, they could not have been so much before, as the sculptors always had the main cave in mind, especially if one remembers that cave excavations were usually conducted in one operation, and if not, left unfinished.

Put all the above evidence against the historical background and the picture is complete. The excavation of the Kailasa could have exhausted any one monarch's resources, and if Kṛṣṇa was engaged on it from his accession in 758 to his death about 773, he cannot have had much money to spare for the Jain temples (which are also obviously later than the colossal monolith he ordered to be excavated), considering also what a devout Hindu he was. His successor, Govinda II, is not known to have been particularly pious, or concerned with much else besides enjoying himself, and Dhruva was for most of his life busy with his northern and southern expeditions.

This brings us to Govinda III (793-814) who had more time for having caves excavated, and to his successsor Amoghavarṣa I (815-878), a monarch of intense Jain conviction. While we hear little of artistic activity in connexion with Govinda, we do know that Amoghavarṣa was a great patron of poetry and learning, and was himself a poet. The fact that he patronized Jain writers suggests that he may have been equally liberal to sculptors and have commissioned them to carve the Ellora Jain caves; it may also be that wealthy Jains had the cave temples chiselled out with that monarch's approval. As Amoghavarṣa's reign extends from the early years of the 9th century to its middle, this view coheres with the recent dating of the Kannada inscriptions (no 7) and leads us to believe that the Rāṣṭrakūṭa caves of the Jain group are indeed of the Jain monarch's days.

As cave temples were quickly started and finished, the sculptors left the cave below the Indra Sabhā only roughly blocked out. This probably occurred after Amoghavarṣa's death in 878. The empire's depleting finances were then put to use in suppressing rebellions or in promoting prestige expeditions north and south, and little was left to provide for temple carving. It was probably in these troubled days that the additional sculptures (with the inscriptions) were executed. These works have a distinct flavour of their own as compared with that of the others—greater rigidity, iconographic simplification and diminished plastic power.

We can here briefly touch on the date of the Chhota Kailasa. Its plan shows that it was probably started not only after the Kailasa was completed, but after the Lankeshvara and the Mother Goddesses as well. If we thus assume that work on the Kailasa was stopped by the third quarter of the eighth century, and that the Lankeshvara-style Jain temples begun in the early years of the ninth, it will be seen that the Lankeshvara would also have been finished before the latter and hence, that the Chota Kailasa is roughly contemporary, its excavation being abandoned at about the same time as that of the lower cave of the Indra Sabhā.

CHAPTER III

THE THEMES OF THE ELLORA SCULPTORS

SECTION 1

BASIC IDEAS OF JAINISM

SECTION 2

THE THEMES OF ELLORA JAIN SCULPTURE

I ENLIGHTENED YOGINS

II ENLIGHTENMENT OF YOGINS

1 Pārśvanātha's Temptation
2 Homage to Bāhubali

III UNIVERSAL DISCOURSE OF THE TĪRTHAṄKARAS

IV SUPERHUMAN BEINGS

1 Sarasvatī
2 Śrī
3 Saudharmendra
4 Sarvānubhūti
5 Gomukha
6 Ambikā
7 Cakreśvarī
8 Padmāvatī
9 Kṣetrapāla
10 Hanumān

V HUMAN ACTIVITIES

1 War : The Rescue of Prasenajit
2 Religious Activities

SECTION 1

BASIC IDEAS OF JAINISM

प्रादेशिकेभ्यः परशासनेभ्यः पराजये यत् तव शासनस्य ।
खद्योतपोतद्युतिडम्बरेभ्यो विडम्बनेयं हरिमण्डलस्य ॥

Hemacandra, *Anyayogavyavacchedikā*, verse 8

This farce of the other confined faiths, overpowering your (universal) Religion, is like that of the clustered gleams of young glowworms overpowering the sun.

The notions of Jainism are intelligible only in the light of the two basic postulates of the Indic religious—*saṁsāra* (the transmigratory world) and *nivṛtti* (liberation).[1] Under these headings come "the four ends of man" of traditional Indian thought—social convention (*dharma*), interest (*artha*), sex (*kāma*) and salvation (*mokṣa*). The first three comprise *saṁsāra* and the fourth is identical with *nivṛtti*. There is however a connexion between these two basic foundational categories—through *dharma*, whose practice lifts a man from the false, passional and transient *saṁsāra*, and keeps him on the path of *mokṣa*.[2]

1. Franklin Edgerton, "Dominant Ideas in the Formation of Indian Culture", *Journal of the American Oriental Society*, vol. 62 (1942), pp. 151 sqq. and A. Guerinot, *Essai de bibliographie Jaina*, Paris 1906, Introduction, p. IX.

2. तथाहि—शुद्धचित्स्वरूपे चरणं चारित्रं, तदेव चारित्रं मिथ्यात्वरागादिसंसरणरूपेण भावसंसारे पतन्तं प्राणिनमुद्धृत्य निर्विकारशुद्धचैतन्ये धरतीति धर्मः ।

Jayasena, *Tātparyavṛtti* on *Pravacanasāra*, *adhyāya* 1, *gāthā* 7, A.N. Upadhye (ed.), *Śrī Kundakundācārya's Pravacanasāra* (*Pavayaṇasāra*), *A Pro-canonical Text of the Jainas... with the Sanskrit commentaries of Amṛtacandra* [*Tattvapradīpikāvṛtti*] *and Jayasena* [*Tātparyavṛtti*], Bombay : Paramaśrutaprabhāvaka-maṇḍala (Sri Rayachandra Jaina Śāstramālā 1935. Jayasena's definition of *saṁsāra* (*adhyāya* 2, *gāthā* 28, p. 169) is worthy of note: संसारः पुनः क्रिया निष्क्रियनिर्विकल्पशुद्धात्मपरिणतेर्विसदृशा मनुष्यादिविभावपर्यायपरिणतिरूपा क्रिया संसाररूपत्वम्।

It is the rendering specific of these broad ideas which gives Jainism, Buddhism and Hinduism their particular character. The texts which define the Jain variants of *saṁsāra* and *nivṛtti* are accepted by all the sects of the religion. This is a great blessing for a student of Jainism, when one considers the difficulties his colleagues in other religions (such as Hinduism and Christianity) have in establishing *their* basic postulates. These texts are Kundakunda's *Pravacanasāra* and Umāsvāti's *Tattvārthādhigamasūtra*.

Three Jain concepts help us to delimit the boundaries of the Jain *saṁsāra* and *nivṛtti*—the living self (*jīva*), the lifeless object (*ajīva*) and activity (*karma*). Activity, which modifies the other two, exists in five states in the living self—influx (*āsrava*), bondage (*bandha*), stoppage (*saṁvara*), gradual dissociation (*nirjara*), and complete elimination in liberation (*mokṣa*).[1]

The living self is essentially consciousness. It has three inherent characteristics: the principle of life, common to all selves; the capacity for salvation, found in some; and the incapacity for salvation, found in others.[2] Jain theologians are not clear if this capacity or incapacity are permanent characteristics; but it would seem that they are only relative, both referring to an *immediate* aptitude for liberation.[3]

Though incorporeal in its pure nature, the living self is identified with a body, which is made up of many "space

1. Pūjyapāda, *Sarvārthasiddhi* [commentary on Umāsvāmi's *Tattvārthādhigamasūtra*], comm. on ch. 1, *Sūtra* 4. S.A. Jain (transl.), *Reality, English Translation of Shri Pūjyapāda's Sarvārthasiddhi*, Calcutta : Vira Sasana Sangha, 1960, p. 7.

2. *Ibid.*

3. "9. The soul whose nature is amenable to modification comes to be auspicious, inauspicious or pure according as it develops auspicious, inauspicious or pure states. . . .

11. The self that has developed equanimity, if endowed with pure activities, attains the bliss of Nirvāṇa, and if endowed with auspicious activities attains heavenly happiness.

12. By the rise of inauspicious activities, the soul wanders for long as a low-graded human being, a sub-human being and a hellish one being subject for ever to thousands of miseries. Upadhye, *op. cit.* p. 2. Transl. of *Pravacanasāra*, *adhyāya* 1, vv. 9, 11, 12.

points" (*pradeśas*). Space as a whole is infinite, filled by numberless indivisible elementary particles (*paramāṇu*); the area that each one of these covers is a space point.[1] According to the numbers of such points at its disposal, the self can expand and contract, like the light of a lamp (in open air or in a room), and thus can occupy a large or small body.[2]

The vibration of the molecules of the body is passed on to the self by virtue of their identification. Just as water flows into a lake through streams, karmic matter enters the soul by means of activity.[3] This brings about Karma's first state, *influx*. Its second state, *bondage*, originates from the first, for, when unhindered, influx causes the self to be born again and again—in other words, to be "bound" to a manifold and miserable existence. The person intent on liberation has to prevent further influx, or bring about its *stoppage*, and then go on to dislodge or gradually dissociate the previously accumulated matter from the self's incorporeal substance, until it is completely separated and its association with the self destroyed. The last two operations are like the cleaning of muddy water. Clearing nuts moved in this water make the mud subside (*dissociation*) and then the clear water is poured into another pot (*liberation*).[4]

With these ideas in mind, we can define the Jain interpretation of *saṁsāra* and *nivṛtti*. *Saṁsāra* is a state of the self with the flux of an unhappy existence caused by karmic matter seeping into the soul. *Nivṛtti* is "the attainment of an altogether different state of the soul, on the removal of all the impurities of karmic matter and the body, characterized by the inherent qualities of the soul such as knowledge and bliss free from pain and suffering."[5]

The uncompromising hostility which Indic theologians often show to *saṁsāra*, in believing its total removal to be

1. *Sarvārthasiddhi*, comm. on ch. V, *sūtra* 8. *Reality*, p. 135.
2. *Ibid.*, comm. on ch. V. *sūtra* 16, *Reality*, p. 141.
3. *Ibid.*, comm. on ch. VI, *sūtra* 2. *Reality*, p. 168.
4. *Ibid.*, comm. on ch. VI, *sūtra* 1, *Reality*, p. 47. For an exposition of Jain Karma doctrine see A.N. Upadhye, "Jainism and Karma Doctrine", *The Jaina Antiquary* II-1 (Jn. 1936), pp. 1-28.
5. *Sarvārthasiddhi*, ch. 1, Introductory passage, *Reality*, p. 2.

essential to *mokṣa*, leaves us with the impression that *saṁsāra* is ineradicably evil; yet our theologians are always finding themselves compelled to admit that there is some good in it. Advaitins, for instance, borrowing an idea from the Sāṅkhyas, postulate a quality of light (*sāttvika*) in the covering of ignorance (*avidyā*) which veils the face of the pure, intelligent and blissful being (*brahman*).[1] The Jains, too, distinguish two kinds of karmas, harmful (*ghāti*) and harmless (*aghāti*). The former comprise knowledge-obscuring, (*jñānāvaraṇīya*), and "faith"-obscuring (*darśanāvaraṇīya*) karmas. The latter are feeling (*vedanīya*) age-determining (*āyus*), body-making (*nāma*) and family-determining (*gotra*) karmas.[2]

When the malignant karmas are destroyed, the pure consciousness of the self is made manifest; so are the qualities of omniscience, eternal happiness, infinite strength and a lustre of extreme brilliance and supersensuousness. All misery is banished, and liberation is attained when the harmless karmas disappear.[3]

Long and tedious lists expand and give further precision to these basic ideas. Among the more attractive of the classifications is that of the souls,[4] which is almost the only one to have a bearing on iconography. There are two broad divisions of souls, the liberated and the transmigratory. The liberated souls, as we noted, are free from all corporeal and passional association. The transmigratory ones, on the other hand, immersed in ignorance and passion, are doomed (according to the meritorious or demeritorious quality of their acts) to experiencing a succession of more or less happy or unhappy conditions of existence. These, in their totality, constitute the form of the universe and are of four kinds—infernal, sub-

1. This *avidyāguṇatrayabheda* produces Viṣṇu, Brahmā and Rudra. See Madhusūdana Sarasvatī, *Siddhāntabindu* on *śloka* 8. Ed. V.S. Abhyankar, Poona : Bhandarkar Oriental Research Institute, 1928, pp. 90-91.

2. *Sarvārthasiddhi*, comm. on ch. VIII, *sūtra* 4. *Reality*, p. 220.

3. Upadhye, *Śrī Kundakundācārya's Pravacanasāra*, Introduction, p.XCII.

4. T. N. Ramachandran, *Tiruparuttikuṇṛam and its Temples* (Bulletin of the Madras Government Museum, III) Madras 1934, Appendix III, pp. 185-235.

human, human and celestial.[1] These beings are coloured, according to the intensity or rarity of passion in them, by a range of hues comprising black, blue, grey, flame colour, lotus pink and white.[2] Some of them have minds, others not. The mind-gifted beings are celestial, human and infernal and also the "higher" animals (ox, horse, monkey, pigeon, serpent etc.); among those lacking a mind are the "lower" animals and lifeless objects. The beings with a mind can distinguish concepts, truth and falsehood, good and evil. They can also preach and be taught. Lower animals cannot do this, but they still have some sort of knowledge and are open to scriptural influence.[3]

1. *Sarvārthasiddhi*, comm. on ch. II, *sūtra* 6. *Reality*, p. 53.
2. *Ibid.*
3. Olivier Lacombe in ch. 12 of *L'Inde classique*, paragraph 2475, p. 652.

SECTION II

THE THEMES OF ELLORA JAIN SCULPTURE

The whole content of the Jain religion can in one way or another be related to the classification of souls, and the range of themes provided is quite vast. Even so the repertory of Ellora Jain sculpture is small. The sculptors avoid the infernal beings and the elaborate Jain cosmology, and confine themselves to the enlightened selves (or yogins) and the superhuman and human beings. From what I have been able to identify of the Ellora sculptures their choice of subjects can be classified schematically under the following heads :

I ENLIGHTENED YOGINS

1 The group of yogins : Pañcaparameṣṭins
2 Ādinātha or Ṛṣabhanātha
3 Śāntinātha
4 Pārśvanātha
5 Supārśva ?
6 Neminātha ?
7 Mahāvīra ?
8 Bāhubali or Gomaṭa

II ENLIGHTENMENT OF YOGINS

1 Pārśvanātha's temptation
2 Homage to Bāhubali

III UNIVERSAL DISCOURSE OF THE TĪRTHAṄKARA

1 The Samavasaraṇa

IV SUPERHUMAN BEINGS

1 Sarasvatī
2 Śrī
3 Saudharmendra
4 Sarvānubhūti

5 Gomukha
6 Ambikā
7 Cakreśvari
8 Padmāvatī
9 Kṣetrapāla
10 Hanumān
11 Śaṅkhanidhi
12 Padmanidhi

V HUMAN ACTIVITIES

1 War
2 Religion

I ENLIGHTENED YOGINS

Enlightenment was attained by the Jain yogins in sitting or standing postures. Though only three tīrthaṅkaras—Ṛṣabha, Neminātha and Mahāvīra—were enlightened whilst seated,[1] the sitting posture is the more popular and is of two kinds. In the first case the foot of only one leg is over the knee of the opposite leg—that is, right foot over left knee, and left foot beneath right knee. This pose is called the "hero" pose (*vīrāsana*) or "half-lotus" pose (*ardhapadmāsana*).[2] The second

1. T. N. Ramachandran, *op. cit.*, p. 191. "The ascetic does not swerve from the path to liberation, nor does his body move from the sitting postures such as *vīrāsana* ...he overcomes the pain caused by continuation in the same posture for a long time." *Sarvārthasiddhi*, comm. on ch. IX, *sūtra* 9, *Reality*, p. 253.

2. *VĪRĀSANA*

एकपादमथैकस्मिन् विन्यस्योरौ च संस्थितः ।
इतरस्मिंस्तदा पादं वीरासनमुदाहृतम् ॥

Pratimāvijñānam, ch. 10, v. 3 in
D. N. Shukla,
Vāstuśāstra, Vol. 2, Chandigarh :
Punjab University 1958, p. 40.

एकत्रोरूणि संस्थाप्य पादमेकमथेतरत् ।
ऊरूं पादे निवेश्यैतद्वीरासनमुदाहृतम् ॥

Ahirbudhnyasaṁhitā, quoted by Gopinātha Rao, *Elements of Hindu Iconography*, vol. I, pt. 1, Madras 1914, p. 18.

type of pose has each foot over the knee of the other leg, and is called "lotus" pose (*padmāsana*).[1] The Southern tradition, inclusive of the Ellora Jain, generally adopts the hero pose; the Northern Indian Jains (like the Ellora Buddhists) employ the lotus pose.

Jain art is concerned mostly with the sitting yogin, with or without iconographical paraphernalia. The standing yogin comes next. His is an erect position, with arms hanging loose by his sides, and is called the "body stretching" pose (*kāyotsarga*)[2]. The arms usually reach down to the knees. The early Jain[3] and all Digambara representations of the standing yogin show him stark naked, or "sky-clad" (see Illustration 1).

Jain doctrine admits five kinds of wise men—and it is often difficult to distinguish between them—who are the "Five Supreme Lords" (Pañcaparameṣṭins):[4]

1 Siddha, the "Realized"
2 Arhat, the "Noble"
3 Ācārya, the Master
4 Upādhyāya, the Teacher
5 Sādhu, the Ascetic.

1. *PADMĀSANA*

ऊरूमूले वामपादं पुनस्तद्दक्षिणं पदम् ।
वामोरौ स्थापयित्वा तु पद्मासनमिदं स्मृतम् ॥

Pratimāvijñānam, ch. 10, v. 1,
Vāstuśāstra, p. 40.

ऊर्वोरुपरि संस्थाप्य उभे पादतले सुखम् ।
पद्मासनमिदं प्रोक्तं सर्वकिल्बिषनाशकम् ॥

Ahirbudhnyasaṁhitā, quoted by Gopinātha Rao, *op. et. loc. cit.*

2. आजानुलम्बबाहुः श्रीवत्साङ्कः प्रशान्तमूर्तिश्च ।
दिग्वासास्तरुणो रूपवांश्च कार्योऽर्हतां देवः ॥

Varāhmihira, *Bṛhatsaṁhitā*,
Benares : Chowkhambā 1959, ed. P. A. Jha, p. 394.

3. U. P. Shah, "Age of Differentiation of Digambara and Śvetāmbara Images and the Earliest known Śvetāmbara Bronzes", *Bulletin of the Prince of Wales Museum of Western India*, no. 1 (1950-1951), pp. 30-40, especially 34.

4. See *Pañcapratikramaṇādisūtra*; Indranandin, *Parameṣṭipūjā*; Hemacandra, *Abhidhānacintāmaṇi*; Amṛtacandrasūri, *Puruṣārthasiddhyupāya*.

Illustration 1
CAVE 32 (J 20) Detail of façade.

[facing p. 38

As we noted above, the selves belong to two categories, the liberated and the bound, and the five supreme ones can be classified under these categories. I Shall Take them In turn :

1. The *Siddha*, the only liberated self from among the five, is himself of two kinds:[1] *Sāmānya Siddha*, who is both liberated and disembodied and *Tīrthaṅkara Siddha*, who is now a *Sāmānya Siddha*, but who when embodied preached the Jain law.

2. The *Arhat*, or the enlightened one still encumbered by the body.[2]

3. The *Ācārya*, the head of a group of sages.[3]

4. The *Upādhyāya*, who studies and teaches the Jain scriptures.[4] (See fig. 1, below, p. 175.)

5. The *Sādhu*, or ascetic.[5]

I have found only one panel where the Supreme Ones are shown together, in the Indra Sabhā at Ellora.[6] In all other cases they are depicted separately. Thus represented, they fall into two groups—the tīrthaṅkara Siddha and the Arhat in the one, and the Ācārya, Upādhyāya and Sādhu in the other. The first two live in the rarified atmosphere of pure contemplation, even when they are in contact with the world; the other three are very much in the world, though endeavouring to free themselves from it. The Tīrthaṅkara and the Arhat thus properly belong to this section, "The Enlightened Yogins"; the others are better dealt with in the last section "Human Activities".

Of the Tīrthaṅkara and Arhat, the former—either because of the sculptors' obsession with this theme, or their inertia or poverty of ideas—is overwhelmingly the main subject of Jain sculpture, for the Tīrthaṅkara especially is supremely 'the embodiment of the path to liberation, as it were indicating

1. T. N. Ramachandran, *op. cit.*, p. 189.
2. *Ibid.*, p. 213.
3. *Ibid.*, p. 214.
4. *Ibid.*, p. 219.
5. *Ibid.*
6. The Indra Sabhā Pañcaparameṣṭī panel was pointed out to me by S. Padmanabha Rao, who was guide-lecturer of the Ellora temples in 1964.

the path by his very form even without uttering words".[1] The Tīrthaṅkara dominates Jain art more than Christ does that of Christianity, the Buddha that of Buddhism, or any god or hero that of his religion and cult. Yet it is not any particular tīrthaṅkara that Jain sculptors seem to be preoccupied with, at least in the Ellora temples—it is the tīrthaṅkara type as such. All the 24 of the tīrthaṅkaras are of a uniform pattern. Their whole history has three main phases. The first comprises their several rebirths leading to the final one. The second comprehends the actions of the last birth preliminary to the art of liberation. The third is the liberation itself.

In the round of rebirths, the tīrthaṅkara sometimes has an enemy, who goes through his own sequence of transmigrations, and torments our hero in each birth. In the tīrthaṅkara's last birth, the enemy makes a last desperate attempt to destroy him but is compelled to realize the futility of his attacks and is converted.

The next two phases of the tīrthaṅkara's life have five auspicious moments (*mahākalyāṇas*) :

a Birth
b Anointment
c Renunciation
d Enlightenment
e Liberation

The first four constitute his birth and life before liberation —our second phase—and the last moment is our third and last phase.

The solemn monotony of the figures in the gloom of the Ellora Jain caves will convince any one of how little the individuality of the tīrthaṅkaras meant to the Jains and their artists. Even in the succeeding centuries, when sculptors acquired a whole iconographical vocabulary enabling them to differentiate between the tīrthaṅkaras' identities, we find little character in the sages' figures. Only symbols tacked on to thrones and pedestals distinguish them,[2] as does the iconographical character of their attendant *yakṣas* and *yakṣīs*.

1. *Sarvārthasiddhi*, ch. I, Introductory passage. *Reality*, p. 1.

2. "Now a study of Jaina iconography has revealed that the recognition symbols (*lāñchhanas*) first appeared in the art of the fifth century when

It is not surprising then if we cannot indicate the identity of more than three tīrthaṅkaras with any certainty—that of Ṛṣabha,[1] Śāntinātha and Pārśvanātha. Ṛṣabha can be made out because of the locks of hair on his shoulder,[2] which he sometimes shares with his son Bāhubali. We need other iconographical signs to separate them, and we find that for Ṛṣabha the sitting pose is necessary and that the three-tiered umbrella of the tīrthaṅkara is a help; for Bāhubali, the creepers entwined round his standing figure are absolutely needful; and the one-tiered umbrella (when shown) confirms that the figure under it is not a tīrthaṅkara.

The second figure, Śāntinātha, is recognized by his symbol, the deer, affixed to his pedestal, in a solitary sculpture of the Yādava group on the other side of the hill (Cāraṇādri). This is a very weak symbol, because Bāhubali also often has a deer standing near; and on a damaged sculpture, where the creepers cannot be made out, and where the umbrella is broken, it would be hard to say whether the sage was Śāntinātha or Bāhubali.

The third of these, Pārśvanātha, is perhaps the most popular of the tīrthaṅkaras and certainly the most striking. It is a relief to see the snake canopy, with its waving lines and curved planes poised over his head, standing out from among the monotonous ranks of the other characterless Jinas.

Here too, the Jina is not left in peaceful possession of his attribute; another tīrthaṅkara appropriates the snake —

the symbol is placed in the centre of the lion seat on either side of the central dharma-chakra while the deer on each side of the wheel is absent." U. P. Shah, "Bronze Hoard from Vasantgarh", *Lalit Kalā*, nos. 1-2 (April 1955-March 1956), p. 59.

1. ṚṢABHA IN POETRY

For Ṛṣabha in Jain devotional poetry see (1) Jinaprabhasūri, *Ṛṣabhajinastavana*; (2) Sāmantabhadra, *Ṛṣabhajinastavana*; (3) Udayasāgara, *Ṛṣabhajinastavana*; (4) Dhanapāla, *Ṛṣabhapañcāśikā*; (5) Jinasundarasūri, *Ṛṣabhastava*; (6) Anon. *Ṛṣabhadevastavana*; (7) Anon. *Ṛṣabhajinastuti*; (8) Anon. *Ṛṣabhajinastuti*. Nos. (1), (2), (3), (7) and (8) are found in *Stotrasamuccaya* or *Jainastotrasamuccaya* ed. Caturvijayamuni, Bombay : Nirnaya Sagara Press 1928; no. (4) in *Kāvyamālā* VII, Bombay : same press 1908; no. (5) in *Jainastotrasaṅgraha*, pt. 2, Bombay : same press 1947; no. (6) in *Saḍbhāṣāmayāni Jinapañcakastotrāṇi*, reference lost.

2. U. P. Shah, *Studies in Jaina Art*, p. 24, footnotes 2, 4, 3.

Supārśva. Both Pārśva's and Supārśva's mothers, before conceiving their sons, saw a snake in a dream; Pārśva also had one standing guard over him at the time he was being enlightened, and a snake hovered over Supārśva when the latter was delivering his first sermon after enlightenment.

Later iconography solved this by prescribing five hoods for Supārśva's snake, and seven for Pārśva's. And though Pārśvanātha was in every way more popular than Supārśva,[1] added to the fact that the former's temptation was a great favourite with the Ellora sculptors, we cannot fully clear the shadow of suspicion which hovers over those tīrthaṅkara figures whose snakes have five hoods.

Later iconographical conventions also make us suspect that some of the tīrthaṅkara figures cannot be Nemināthas, particularly those in the temple shrines. According to subsequent Digambara ideas, the *yakṣa* of Neminātha was Sarvāhna or Sarvānubhūti; and his *yakṣī*, Ambikā[2]—the couple always either found before the Ellora sanctums, or architecturally juxtaposed with them. However this couple (particularly the *yakṣī*) are elsewhere seen to accompany other tīrthaṅkaras.[3] Later prescriptions of a fixed couple do not seem to have become established before the eleventh century, and there is at least one example of an attempt to combine the new convention with the old one, where, accompanying an image of Ṛṣabha, the bull face of his new *yakṣa* Gomukha is superimposed on the body of the old Sarvānubhūti.[4]

The last of the possible identifications is Mahāvīra, the twenty-fourth tīrthaṅkara.[5] This does not seem to have any

1. U. P. Shah, *op. cit.*, p. 12, footnote 1.
2. T. N. Ramachandran, *op. cit.*, pp. 195 and 208-209.
3. For instance, Ambikā accompanies Ṛṣabha (Lilvādeva bronzes), Pārśvanātha (Ellora, Lilvādeva), Neminātha (later iconography) and even Mallinātha and Śāntinātha. See U. P. Shah "Iconography of the Jain Goddess Ambikā", pt. 2. *Journal of the University of Bombay*, IX (Sept. 1940), p. 166.
4. *Lalit Kalā*, nos. 1-2, fig. 19.
5. Fergusson and Burgess, *The Cave Temples of India*, London 1880, pt. II, bk IV, ch. III, pp. 497 *sqq.* R. S. Gupta and B. D. Mahajan, *Ajanta, Ellora and Aurangabad Caves*, Bombay : D. B. Taraporevala Sons & Co., Private Ltd., 1962. pp. 220 *et passim.*

iconographical foundation. Its one justification is that people assume that the historical founder of Jainism cannot be left unrepresented in the temples; they then suppose that he must occupy the most prominent place—the sanctum. Working outwards from this, and following the prescriptions of later iconography, some of them identify the attendant *yakṣī* as Siddhāyikā and the *yakṣa* as Mātaṅga.[1] However, many of the Jain structural temples accommodate all kinds of tīrthaṅkaras in their shrines, just as the main altars of the churches of Christendom are thrones for every sort of saint. I myself have never seen any image of Mahāvīra, at least in the Digambara tradition, accompanied by Ambikā and Sarvānubhūti, and the fact that this couple is found before the Ellora shrines casts even greater doubt on the Mahāvīra identification.

The tīrthaṅkara image is made up of the figure of the tīrthaṅkara and the eight *prātihāryas*. The latter spontaneously come into existence at the time of enlightenment, with the destruction of two types of obstructive *ghāti karmas*, those of enjoyment and re-enjoyment; with the destruction of the first type, there is a shower of flowers etc.; with the annihilation of the second, the throne, fans, three umbrellas and other splendours are manifested.[2]

Next to the Tīrthaṅkara in importance is the Arhat. The only individual of this type which the Ellora sculptors are concerned with is Ṛṣabha's proud son, Bāhubali, who renounced world sovereignty for enlightenment, this renunciation being a favourite theme of the sculptors. He is frequently shown with other figures arranged to form a patterned motif. But it was also usual to carve the Arhat by himself, as a standing figure with creepers twining round him. Pārśvanātha too obtained enlightenment whilst standing and he and Bāhubali are often juxtaposed in our temples. Symbolizing the moments of enlightenment of the Tīrthaṅkara (Pārśva) and the Arhat (Bāhubali), these episodes constitute the most popular of the dramatic themes of Ellora Jain sculpture.

1. *Ibid.*, p. 221 *et passim*, where she is often called "Siddhaiki".
2. *Sarvārthasiddhi*, comm. on ch. II, *sūtra* 4. *Reality*, pp. 50-51.

II ENLIGHTENMENT OF YOGINS

1 *Pārśvanātha's temptation*[1]

Of all the themes represented by the Ellora Jain sculptors, Pārśvanātha's temptation is one which offers Jain *Kāvya* some of its choicest opportunities for colour and drama.[2] It satiates the Jain yearning for *śānta* by offering for its delight that emotion in its most vivid form—through its essential quality heightened by contrast with a particularly tumultuous *raudra*.

The main actors in this episode are Pārśva himself, the demon Meghamālin and the serpent Dharaṇendra. The lives of the first two run parallel, from the former's first birth as Marubhūti and the latter's as Kamaṭha. The serpent only appears during Pārśvanātha's final existence.

1. PĀRŚVANĀTHA'S TEMPTATION IN *KĀVYA*.
In Jinasena, *Pārśvābhyudaya*; Bhāvadevasūri, *Pārśvanāthacarita*; Hemavijayagaṇin, *Pārśvanāthacarita*; Bhadrabāhu, *Upasargastava* and Hemacandra, *Triṣaṣṭiśalākāpuruṣacarita*, bk IX, ch. 2, vv. 247-310. transl. Helen Johnson, *Gaekwad Oriental Series* no. 139, vol. V (1962), pp. 394-397.

2. PARŚVANĀTHA IN JAIN DEVOTIONAL LITERATURE
(1) Vādideva Sūri, *Pārśvadharaṇoragendrastavana*; (2) Abhayadeva Sūri, *Pārśvajinacintāmaṇistuti*; (3) Uttamasāgara, disciple of, *Pārśvajināṣṭaka*; (4) Padmaprabhadeva, *Pārśvajināṣṭaka*; (5) Bilhaṇa Kavi *Pārśvajinastava*; (6) Ratnaśekhara Sūri, *Pārsvajinastava*; (7) Vijayasūri Rājaguru, *Pārśvajinastavana*, (8) Jainacandra, *Pārśvajinastavana*; (9) Sakalacandra *Pārśvanāthajinastavana*; (10) Dharmavijaya *Pārśvanāthāṣṭaka*; (11) Sūracandra Sūri, *Pārśvanāthastava*; (12) Jinaprabha Sūri, *Pārśvanāthastavana*; (13) Jinasundara Sūri, *Pārśvanāthastavana*; Padmaprabha Deva, *Pārśvanāthastotra*; (14) Ratnaśekhara Sūri, *Pārśvastavacūri*. The following are anonymous poems : (15) *Pārśvajināṣṭaka*; (16) *Pārśvajinastava*; (17) *Pārśvajinastavana*; (18) *Pārśvajinastotra* (19) *Pārśvalaghustava*; (20) *Pārśvanāthacaityavandana*; (21) *Pārśvanāthastava*; (22) *Pārśvanāthasya mantrādhirājastotram*; (23) *Pārśvanāthavratakathā*. Nos. (1), (3) (6), (7), (9), (14), (17), and (18) are in the *Stotrasamuccaya* (see note 108); nos. (2) and (15) in the *Prācīnajainastotrasaṅgraha*, Agra 1923; nos. (4), (5), (8), (10), (13), and (16) in the *Jainastotrasaṅgraha* (see note 108) ; nos. (11), (19) and (21) in the *Stotraratnākara*, Bombay : Nirnaya Sagara Press 1913-1914, 2 parts; no (12) in *Kāvyamālā* VII (see note 108); nos (20) and (22) in the *Nityasmaraṇastotrasaṅgraha*, Ahmedabad 1919; and no (23) in the *Jinasatyanārāyaṇapūjākathā*, Bombay : Nirnaya Sagara Press, 1908.

In each of these births[1] Kamaṭha murdered Marubhūti. In the latter's last birth as Pārśva, the future tīrthaṅkara (recently married to a girl called Prabhāvatī, whose father he had helped) was looking over Benares from his palace terrace. He saw people hurrying to a spot outside the city with baskets of flowers for offerings, for an ascetic called Kaṭha (who was none other but Kamaṭha himself), was performing the five-fire penance. Through his penetrating knowledge, Pārśva saw that one of the logs blazing in the fire pit held a live serpent. The ascetic denied this, and was proved ignorant when the serpent was extricated: then Kaṭha's pride as all-knowing sage was wounded. Dying full of hate some time after, he was reborn as the demon Meghamālin.

Pārśva returned to his palace, and experienced the joys of love with his wife till they tired him; he then sought initiation as a monk. After a period of wandering he came to a hermitage at sunset and stood motionless under the shadow of a banyan tree. The period which was to end in his full enlightenment had dawned.

Meghmālin had not forgotten his past rancour for Pārśva, and was not going to leave him in peace. He moved to the attack like an elephant rushing to split a mountain. The memory of his former hostility fanned his anger to a great heat, causing it to boil like the ocean with submarine fire. Out of nowhere he conjured up tigers with flaming yellow eyes, saw-like teeth and hook-shaped claws. They lashed the ground with their tails, and their roars sounded like charms of death. Then elephants, looking like live mountains, stampeded trumpeting towards him, their foreheads dripping ichor and their trunks raised to strike. Next came growling bears and a horde of panthers like an army of the god of death. Serpents who burnt trees at a glance flew at him, and after them came vampires armed with knives, looking like clouds with lightning. Their tongues hung out, and flames darted out of their mouths; their huge genitalia made them seem trees with hanging snakes, and their long hands and feet appeared as if mounted on the palm trunks of their legs. A number of them converged to attack Pārśva like dogs an elephant.

1. Hemacandra, *op. cit.*, pp. 356-377.

But just as the ocean on no account stirs from its boundary, nothing could shift Pārśva from his meditation. He was absorbed in it as in a pool of nectar. Soon the animals and fiends, their assaults ineffective, vanished. Meghamālin, now deeply angered, prepared to launch his last attack. From clouds dark as the night of doomsday flashed lightning terrifying as a tongue of Death. The rain hammered the earth like pestles, scourged it like bundles of arrows and dug it up as if with spades. Gripped by confusion, the birds flew wildly up and down the trees and the animals ran this way and that in bewilderment. The floods carried away trees and live animals, and the tīrthaṅkara himself began to be slowly submerged.

Unaffected, he continued to stay quite still, like a jewelled pillar. The waves came up to his ankles, then to his knees and afterwards to his neck. At this moment his dark face was reflected in the expanse of water and looked like a great blue lotus, unruffled and still.

The serpent in the burning log, reborn as the snake king, now started to see what was happening. With his snake-wives he rushed to the rescue, and placing a tall lotus with an erect stalk beneath Pārśva's feet (see Illustration 2), himself covered the tīrthaṅkara with his crown of hoods and his twisted coils (see Illustration 3). His wives danced round the sage, who was however indifferent to everything—to the dance, to his friend Dharaṇa and to his dedicated foe Meghamālin. As the latter continued to shower rain, the snake king looked up in the direction of the demon and threatened to kill him if the rain did not stop. Frightened, Meghamālin ran to Pārśva for refuge, bowed before his feet and craved forgiveness. Then, both the converted enemy and the pleased friend left. Day began to dawn.

Such is the episode as related by Hemacandra, who gave Jain mythology its definitive *kāvya* form.

2 *Homage To Bāhubali*[1]

The meditating Bāhubali is in every way qualified to attract

1. TEXTS ON BĀHUBALI:

(1) Jinasena *Mahāpurāṇa*. Pannalal Jain (ed.), *Mahāpurāṇa ...of Bhagavat Jinasenācārya (Jñānapīṭha Mūrtideva Jaina Granthamālā. Sanskrita Grantha,*

Illustration 2
CAVE 32 (J 18-(16)), Indra Sabhā
Detail of pillar, showing Pārśvanātha on a large lotus.
C. A. D. 810-880

[facing p. 46

Illustration 3
J 27-3. Pārśvanātha-on-the-hill, head of the *tīrthaṅkara.*
Dated A.D. 1234-1235.

[facing p. 47

the artist. He was an extraordinarily handsome young man,[1] a "god of love" (*kāmadeva*), and "beautiful without ornaments".* A nude body like his would thus have for Jain sculptors the allure that the figure of St. Sebastian has for the Christian. The creepers provided an opportunity for covering it with pattern and arabesque, thus to contrast the broad and

No. 8) Kashi : Bhāratīya Jñānapīṭha, 1951, 2 parts (*Ādi* and *Uttara purāṇas*); the Bāhubali text occurs in *Uttarapurāṇa*, *parvas* 35-36, esp. 36, pp. 200-220.

(2) Puṣpadanta, *Mahāpurāṇa*, *sandhi* XVIII, vol. I. pp. 295-305. P. L. Vaidya (ed.), the *Mahāpurāṇa* or *Tisaṭṭhimahāpurisaguṇālaṁkāra* (*A Jain Epic in Apabhraṁśa of the 10th century*) of *Puṣpadanta* (Manikchand Digambara Jaina Granthamala Nos. 37, 41, and 42) Bombay : Manikchand Digambara Jaina Granthamala, 3 vols., vol. I, (1937), vol. 2 (1940), vol. 3 (1941).

(3) Svayambhūdeva, *Paumacariya*, *sandhi* 4. Harivallabh C. Bhayani (ed.), *Paumacariya of Kavirāja Svayambhudeva* (Singhi Jain Series, 34), Bombay: Singhi Jain Sastra Shikshapith, Bharatiya Vidya Bhavan 1953-1960. 3 vols.; vol. 1 (1953), vol. 2 (1953), vol. 3 (1960).

(4) Hemacandra, *op. cit.*, Johnsons' transl. bk. I, ch. V, vv. 519-798, pp. 308-326.

(5) Boppaṇa Paṇḍita, in *Epigraphia Carnatica* (revised by Narasimhachar) II, *Inscriptions at Sravana Belgola* (Revised Edition, Bangalore 1923), pp. 97-100 (original in Kannada). The following are texts to which I have not been able to refer: *Vasudevahiṇḍi*; *Āvaśyaka Niryukti* 322; Haribhadra's *Āvaśyakavṛtti* on *Āvaśyaka Niryukti*; *Āvasyakacūrṇi*; and Doddaiyya's *Bhujabaliśataka*. The following are Kannada works : Pañcabāṇa, *Bhujabalicarita*; Anantakavi, *Gommaṭeśvaracarita*; Devacandra, *Rājāvalikathā*; and the *Sthalapurāṇa* of Shravana Belgola. Some of these references have been got from U. P. Shah, "Bāhubali : A Unique Bronze in the Museum", *Bulletin of the Prince of Wales Museum of Western India*, no 4 (1953-1954), pp. 32-39.

1. Or Gomaṭa, from the Konkani *gomṭo* : अघर कोङ्कणी और मराठी का उद्गम क्रमश: अर्धमागधी और महाराष्ट्री प्राकृत से प्रकट है और यह विदित है कि मराठी, कोङ्कणी एवं कन्नड भाषाओं का शब्द विनिमय पहले होता रहता था ; क्योंकि इन भाषाभाषी देशों के लोगों का पारस्परिक सम्बन्ध विशेष था । अब कोङ्कणी भाषा में एक शब्द 'गोमटो' या 'गोम्मटो' मिलता है और यह संस्कृत के 'मन्मथ' शब्द का रूपान्तर है । और अद्यापि 'सुन्दर' अर्थ में व्यवहृत है । कोङ्कणी भाषा का यह शब्द मराठी भाषा में पहुंच कर कन्नड भाषा में प्रवेश कर गया हो तो कोई आश्चर्य नहीं ।

M. Govind Pai, श्रीबाहुबली की मूर्ति गोम्मट क्यों कहलाती है ? *Jaina Antiquary* vol. IV-2 (1917), p. 108.

* The word *Gomaṭo* (गोमटो), in Konkani, means "beautiful, handsome".

smooth skin texture and the loosely sinuous lines of the human figure with the exiguous forms and elaborate convolutions of the plant. The spirit of the theme, or what Bāhubali (literally) stood for, was also of great fascination. As Hemacandra says, he looked as if he were the very incarnation of the emotion of tranquillity (*śānta rasa*), which, for facial expression, is the prime *rasa* of Indian sculpture (see Illustration 4).

This theme, which inspired sculptors to carve the greatest standing monolithic statue in the world, also furnished *kāvya* writers with imaginative prospects. Not all the life of Bāhubali did so, however, but only the last two of its following three phases. The first of these stretches from his birth to the moment when he realized the vanity of things. The second covers his one year of lone meditation. The third comprises the visit of his brother, Bharata, or his two sisters,[1] which coincided with his enlightenment. Sculpture frequently shows the second phase, and (in Ellora) depicts the third in larger and more monumental panels.[2] The interest of the poets (especially Jinasena) is focused on the moments before the meditation, and on the meditation itself. I shall now describe these phases in greater detail.

Ṛṣabha, the first tīrthaṅkara, had two wives (before he became enlightened), and a hundred sons. Of his first wife Sumaṅgalā he had Bharata, the future world ruler; of the second, Sunandā, Bāhubali was born.

After many victorious battles, Bharata defeated his enemies and, greedy for more land, asked his ninety-nine brothers to give him the territories left to them by their father. All but Bāhubali submitted and became Jain monks. Up to here the various sectarian versions correspond. What follows is in accordance with the account of Jinasena,[3] the Jain *puranist* and poet

1. "Earlier Digambara tradition does not refer to this mission of the two sisters. According to it the defilement (of pride) and dejection (*saṁkleśa*) which prevented Bāhubalī's attainments of the highest knowledge was removed when, at the end of one year, Bharata came and paid his respects to the sage". U. P. Shah, *op. cit.*, p. 33.

2. Of which, perhaps, the Jagannātha Sabhā panel is the most striking.

3. Jinasena, *op. cit.*, *parva* 36.,

Illustration 4
CAVE 32 (J 14-6). Homage to Bāhubali (Gomaṭa).
C. A. D. 810-880.

[facing p. 48

of Amoghavarṣa who probably commissioned the excavation of our temples.

Bharata then marched against Bāhubali and their armies came face to face. The ministers were disturbed by what they saw. This was no war to bring peace, they felt. The leaders were two of the highest beings, so no harm would come to them, but the others would be pitilessly destroyed. Why not let them both fight it out and decide who was to be the world-emperor?

The combat was to be divided into three contests—staring, dousing, and boxing. Bāhubali easily outstared his brother, and then both went to a pond for the next contest. The contestants had to splash water on each other, and the one to be overwhelmed by the other's splashes would lose. Here Bāhubali's greater height stood him in good stead, for while the jets he flung at his brother overpowered him, the splashes from Bharata did not come up even to Bāhubali's face.

They then went on to wrestle. Here too Bāhubali was victorious; after some bouts, he lifted Bharata on to his shoulder, and the bystanders felt they were looking at the Himālaya being hauled up on Nīlagiri—for Bharata was fair and Bāhubali dark.

Blinded with fury, the emperor's eyes rolled in anger. He thought of only one thing—how to avenge his outraged pride. Brushing aside all the rules of the contest, he flung his discus at his brother, but far from striking him down it only circled him and bounced back to its owner. Bāhubali then rushed towards Bharata, and lifting him up once more put him down again. The elder's humiliation was complete.

At this moment, Bāhubali was suddenly overwhelmed by the futility of it all, sovereignty, world, existence and everything. He saw that the yearning for imperial power, the cause of such shame to his brother, could not be anything but a source of misery, and was impermanent anyhow. Sovereignty was like an unfaithful wife who abandoned her husband for other men. As the creeper of royal power was thorny, he would seek the thornless imperium of asceticism.

With these thoughts he went to a forest, where he stood motionless, his arms hanging loosely down his sides. Creepers covered him and serpents, with hoods flared, crawled round him, making him look horrific. The breaths of the serpent young at his feet coalesced to form the illusion of a dark poisonous shoot. But the fire of their breathing was cooled by the power of his calm. His long black locks fell on his shoulders, giving him the appearance of a sandalwood tree fringed with black serpents. The flowering spring creeper embraced him like a loving woman, and when its leaves were plucked away by the *vidyādharīs* it looked again like a woman sorrow-stricken at her lord's feet.

Emaciated as Bāhubali himself was through lack of food, he looked as if he were exhausted through satisfying the woman liberation. Yet not only was his body reduced, his karmas were too. The fire of his concupiscence, which had been fed by the fuel of sense objects, was put out by penance, and the categories of being began to be visible to him in sharp definiteness. It was as if his mind were a room lit by the lamp of knowledge revealing everything in its brilliance, including his karmas, which were as lampblack. The cleansing of his knowledge was accompanied by an ever greater purifying of his asceticism, for penance is to knowledge what a root is to a tree.

Effulgent from his austerities—like a sun emerging from a cloud—with its own rays—his dark body cast over the jungle the radiance of a blue jewel. The wild animals, both the harmless and the preying ones, rested at his feet in tranquillity and affection. The tigress licked the heads of the young of buffaloes as if they were her own. Lionesses suckled young elephants, and cow-elephants the lion cubs.

Wishing to clear the space in front of the sage, elephants sprinkled it with water brought in lotus petals. Clusters of lotuses were placed at his feet; the glow of the masses of dark serpents there made them look like garlands of blue lotuses offered to the arhat. Creepers weighed down with brilliant flowers, appeared to be devotees bowed with offerings.

The whole jungle seemed to do a dance out of joy and devotion, the ever-flowering trees swaying in the wind, the serpents with their gem-flashing hoods moving to the murmur of the bees, and the peacocks to the notes of the koels. The greatness of this fully tranquil sage brought down a calm on the jungle. *Vidyādharas* constantly alighted from their chariots to honour the

heavens without respite. *Vidyādharīs* would come down to enjoy themselves by plucking away the creepers entwined round his body.

Bāhubali came nearer and nearer to full enlightenment but was kept back from the climax by one obstruction: sorrow at having humiliated his brother. But Bharata was himself now thoroughly repentant of his wicked move to strike Bāhubali down, and came back in a year, on the day of his brother's renunciation, to do him homage, with his priests, ministers, kings, court and women. Ganges water was poured out, jewel lamps were lit, incense made of wishing-tree wood was burnt, offerings of *pārijāta* and other divine flowers were made, and other lavish ceremonies performed.

The sight of his brother's happiness and reparation removed Bāhubali's last obstacle. Full enlightenment flashed on him; the gods' thrones trembled, bringing Indra and others down to worship; winds wafted down heavenly flowers and the spray from the agitated waves of the Ganges of the sky; the drums of the gods sounded in the heavens; a jewelled umbrella was contrived by divine artisans in the sky, and beneath it, a shining throne. Of themselves, fly whisks hovered at his sides, and the ground for his discourse also appeared. A great concourse of eager yogīs clustered around him, making him look like a moon encircled by stars.

It is interesting to compare Jinasena's account with a Kannada poem of Boppaṇa Paṇḍita—another text of the southern Digambara tradition, composed around 1180, on the Gomaṭa monolith of Śravaṇa Belgola.[1] The reason for Gomaṭa's not attaining enlightenment quickly is given as pride, not sorrow; and reluctance to stand on any part of Bharata's domain. Realizing this, the latter says to him, "Give up the idea that your feet are in my territory; when one thinks of it, the territory is neither yours nor mine". Bharata later made a colossal image of his brother, in an area which became first infested with *kukkuṭasarpas*, or "cock-serpents" (and came to be called *kukkuṭeśvara*), and then invisible to the carnal eye. The colossus of Śravaṇa Belgola was carved as a substitute, as a "Southern *kukkuṭeśvara*".

1. Boppaṇa Paṇḍita, *op. et. loc. cit.*

Boppaṇa's text has some striking images. The three worlds are together Gomaṭa's abode—the serpents form its foundation, the earth its base, the points of the compass its walls, the chariots of the gods its towers and the clusters of stars its inner jewelled awning. The gods showered brilliant white flowers, like so many stars, on Gomaṭa's lovely head when he won both his wrestling contest and his struggle against Karma. They still occasionally do so on his statue, for a whole day; and it is a sight which delights women, children, old people and cowherds. What is the point of adoring the dying gods of the land (which only takes one deeper into the forest of births) when the contemplation of Gomaṭa rids one of birth, old age, and other sorrows ? For he is indeed the form of the supreme soul, one who abandoned his two empires of desire (as Cupid incarnate) and the world (as victor over Bharata) for that of emancipation.[1]

We cannot end our examination of this theme without also seeing what Hemacandra[2] has to say about it. As voicing the views of the Śvetāmbara sect, he gives an account which differs in several details from Jinasena's. The second contest, according to Hemacandra, is not a water fight, but a voice fight, where the parties have to out-shout each other. Here again Bāhubali wins; his voice grows louder, while that of his brother, weaker and weaker. The last fight is not just boxing and wrestling but a sort of fencing with wooden staffs as well.

When the discus is flung at him and bounces back to Bharata, Bāhubali is in such a rage that he runs to kill Bharata, and is suddenly struck with shame at the thought. He then becomes a monk on spot, tearing his hair out (as Jain monks do at initiation) like so many tufts of grass. He stands quite still on the battlefield itself and does his penance there, deciding not to go to his brothers for fear of being thought inferior to them because of his later choice of the path of deliverance. He plans to visit them after enlightenment. This is how Hemacandra describes Bāhubali's penance:

"The blessed muni, Bāhubali, remained there alone, as if sprung from the earth, as if fallen from the sky. Devoted to

1. See also *Epigraphia Carnatica*, *tom. cit.*, p. 145.
2. Hemacandra, *op. et. loc.* cit.

meditation, his eyes fixed on the end of his nose, motionless, the muni appeared like a sign-post. Like a forest tree, his body endured the wind in the hot season spreading hot grains of sand like grains of fire. Plunged in the nectar of good meditation, he was unconscious of the sun in the middle of the hot season, like a fire pit, over his head. Covered from head to foot with mud made from dust and perspiration caused by the heat, he looked like a boar that had come out of mud. In the rainy season he was no more disturbed by streams of water, than a mountain by trees shaken by wind and rain. He was not shaken from kāyotsarga nor from meditation by the flashes of lightning nor by the mountatin peaks shaken by thunder-storms. Both of his feet were covered with moss caused by dripping water, like the steps of a deserted village-tank. In the winter season in which elephant-deep streams were frozen he remained comfortable from the fire of meditation active in burning the fuel of karma. On winter nights when trees were frozen by cold, Bāhubali's pious meditation bloomed especially, like jasmines (which flower during winter in India).

Forest buffaloes scratched themselves on him just as on the trunk of a huge tree, at the same time splitting their horns. Families of rhinoceroses experienced the delight of sleep at night resting with their bodies on his body, just as on a mountain side. Elephants pulling at his hands and feet with the idea they were olibanum-shoots, were often embarrassed, unable to pull them up. Herds of yaks, their faces upturned, licked him fearlessly with tongues that were dreadful from their rough surfaces like saws. He was surrounded completely by creepers with a hundred branches shooting up, like a drum with leather thongs. Dense clusters of reeds grew up and around him, which had the appearance of quivers filled with arrows that had come from the power of former affection. Abundant darbha-grass filled with moving centipedes grew up around his feet buried in the mud of the rainy season. Hawks, sparrows, etc., in harmony with each other, made nests on his body covered with creepers. Thousands of serpents hid in the thickets of creepers, terrified by the call of the forest peacocks. Bāhubali looked as if he had a thousand arms from hanging serpents fastened to his body. His feet were surrounded by serpents, like anklets that had left the ant-hill near his feet. As he stood thus in meditation, a year passed without food. . ."[1]

When the year was nearing its end, Ṛṣabha realized that it was pride which kept enlightenment from his son, so he sent his daughters, the nuns Brāhmī and Sundarī, to point out the fact to him. When the women arrived at the spot of his penance, they could not discover where he was, so completely had the creepers covered him, like dust a jewel. When they finally found him, they said, cryptically: "Enlightenment does not arise in those seated on an elephant's shoulder", and off they went. Bāhubali realized that by "elephant" they meant "pride". He then decided to go and pay homage to his father and brothers. He had but taken a step, when full enlightenment possessed him, and his destructive karmas snapped like a row of creepers.[2]

III UNIVERSAL DISCOURSE OF THE TĪRTHAṄKARAS

The Samavasaraṇa

On the Tīrthaṅkara's enlightenment, the eight wondrous things make their appearance, as does the ground for his first discourse (*sabhāvvāṇi*). This happened to Bāhubali, too, according to Jinasena, but nobody insisted on his preaching, so the enlightened sage did not become a tīrthaṅkara. In the case of the men who have the honour to become that, the gods at once set about erecting a mammoth assemblage of structures for the audience, which is called *samavasaraṇa*. Jinasena describes it in lavish detail, devoting 241 verses to it alone in his 22nd *parva*. He conceives it as a vast circular area with the temple of discourse in the centre, and the whole plan radiating outwards from it in four concentric walls. The innermost is that of crystal, next of silver, the third of gold and the last of jewel dust.

The central circle has the temple of discourse, Śrī Maṇḍapa, with three platforms, one above the other. The lowest is of lapis lazuli, the midmost of gold, and the third of assorted jewels. On this is erected the pavilion Gandhakuṭi, which has

1. *Ibid.*, pp. 324-325.
2. *Ibid.*, pp. 325-326.

golden lattice work, pearl festoons hanging from pinnacles, and is adorned with numerous banners. In the pavilion is a jewel lion-throne, lovelier than mount Meru itself, on which sits the tīrthaṅkara, showered with flowers by the gods. Near him is the aśoka tree, and over his head the triple umbrella. Sixty four yakṣas wave fly-whisks at his sides, and an orb of light glows behind him. Celestial drum music sounds from the sky.

From the Śrī Maṇḍapa begin avenues which go to the gateways at the four points of the outer wall. Immediately around the central building are nine lofty *stupas* in the centre of the avenues, and on the avenues' sides are balconied residences, town halls, theatres and rest houses. This built-up area is encircled by a ring of doorways, which open out on parks.

From here to the crystal wall a fixed pattern is adhered to; beyond the crystal wall are the spaces between the other two ramparts of silver and gold. There are parks, jars of incense and dance halls flanking the road. There are differences in the sort of trees confined to each park, the ornamentation of the ramparts and such things. When one comes to the gateway of the gold rampart one sees the moat that runs around it. It is filled with lotuses, and has islands with creeper groves and pleasure hills.

The road over this moat leads to the jewel dust wall. But before one gets to its arched entrance one sees the towering *māna stambhas*, "pride pillars" as imposing as the quarter elephants themselves, standing on three tiers of pillars, adorned with flags and bells and surrounded by three walls. At their feet are images of tīrthaṅkaras worshipped to the accompaniment of music and dancing. On their four sides are step-wells of precious stones, also bright with lotuses. The whole area of this complex is itself of blue gems. Around it is the irridescent rainbow glow arising from the particles making up the wall of jewel dust.

There is considerable variation in Digambara and Śvetāmbara accounts, but they agree in the broad outline of the plan —a central pavilion for the discourse on a large platform, from which radiate three concentric walls with four gateways in four directions. Originally the plan was conceived as circular (being based on the stūpa) and later as a square. Into this area, beings of three conditions of existence were allowed—celestial, human and subhuman. Hemacandra says that the gods made three images of the tīrthaṅkara, and placed them in the other directions, so that all could see the sage preaching. Later works on the *samavasaraṇa* become text books of a celestial ceremonial overwhelmingly rigorous and exacting. It is relevant for us only to note that Indra begins the proceedings with a hymn of praise to the tīrthaṅkara, and often dances out of joy at its end.[1]

IV *Superhuman Beings*

Superhuman beings are those who move freely in the terrestrial world and derive pleasure in several parts of it. They are endowed with magnificence, splendour and extraordinary powers.[2] There are at least four kinds of them:

1 Mansion dwelling (*bhavanavāsi*)
2 Peripatetic (*vyantara*)
3 Stellar (*jyotiṣka*)
4 Chariot dwelling (*vaimānika*).

This list is fixed in Jain theology, but leaves out some of the important gods worshipped by the Jains. The chief types of the above four represented in our temples are the peripatetic and chariot-dwelling gods. Under the former class fall the *yakṣas*,[3] who are distinguished from the other superhuman beings in that they are "tree-addicts", so to speak. The latter class is represented by the chariot-dweller Saudharmendra in the Ellora sculptures.

These gods have their places in the vast universe projected by the Jain imagination. This universe is like the figure of a man standing with arms akimbo, and resembles a cane stand at its top, a cymbal in its centre and a drum at its bottom. Its entire fabric is swathed in three wind sheaths—thick,

1. For other treatments of the *samavasaraṇa* see *Paumacariya* 3, 4-12; *Āvaśyakasūtra*; *Vividhatīrthakalpa*.

2. *Sarvārthasiddhi*, Comm. on ch. IV, *sūtra* 1. *Reality*, p. 107.

3. S. K. Jaini, "Some Common Elements in the Jaina and Hindu Pantheons, I. Yakshas and Yakshiṇis", *The Jaina Antiquary* XVIII-2 (Dec. 1952), pp. 32-35 and XIX-1 (Jn. 1953), pp. 21-23.

medium and rare—which envelop the universe like bark a tree. Through its centre runs a region of live souls, which is called its nerve or cord, the channel of the world tree's sap.

The lower world is made up of seven earths, one on top of the other, each of them supported by three atmospheres—gross air, vapour, and thin air. These earths have each their own pigment: jewel hue, and of sugary, sandy, miry, smoky, dark and pitchy colour. In these regions live the infernal beings, tormentors and tormented. The former, who are fiends (*asuras*) make their victims drink molten iron, embrace red-hot iron pillars, climb up and down thorn trees; they smash others with hammers, cut them with hatchets and knives, sprinkle boiling oil on them, fry them in an iron vessel, roast them in an oven, drown them in the hell river and crush them in an oil press. As the lives of the damned cannot be cut short, all this mauling does not kill them. They are not friends among themselves either, for they are always going for one another like dogs and jackals, striking, biting and cutting one another open with all kinds of weapons. In this region too, in its jewelled and miry parts, live most of the peripatetic gods.

The middle world is a circular body of concentric rings, with outer, inner and middle divisions. The inner division consists of sixteen continents. Its centre is a mighty circular continent —ours—Jambūdvīpa, surrounded by the others in rings, each divided from its neighbour by ring-shaped oceans. This is the world of men. In its centre, that is, in mid-Jambūdvīpa, rises the Meru mountain, a truncated cone of gold and gems several million miles high, its foot and terraced sides ringed with dense groves.

There are innumerable scattered islands off these continents, on which live the barbarians, who are a funny lot, some with tails, others with horns, hare-like ears; with faces of dog, horse, buffalo, pig, tiger, crow and monkey, some even with a single thigh. Several barbarians live on the continents too, such as the Ionians, foresters and mountain men, who dwell on the fringe of the Aryan world of which Bhārata (or India) is a part.

The upper world is a sequence of palatial chariots one overtopping another, and also serried circles of heavenly bodies, rotating round the Meru mountain in which the stellar deities live. In the palatial chariots, some of which are known as the *kalpas*, dwell a concourse of gods each headed by a lord or Indra. The first of these chariots, the Saudharma Kalpa, is only a hair's breadth above Meru; its chief is Saudharmendra, the lord of Saudharma. Presumably because his heaven is the nearest to the earth, Saudharmendra takes part in all the important events of a tīrthaṅkara's life.

The other heavens not only arise in a linear succession above the Saudharma Kalpa, but also extend in four directions among the stars that are scattered like flowers in the intermediate points of the compass.

Among the chief unclassified heavenly beings are Sarasvatī and Śrī, the former being the most important goddess for the Jain monk, as symbolizing the speech of the tīrthaṅkaras; and the latter, for the Jain layman, (who is member of a prosperous community) as personifying wealth. However, both appear very seldom in our temples: the place of the former is more than adequately filled by the tīrthaṅkaras themselves, and that of the latter is occupied by a figure who is nearer in appearance to the Jain businessman than Śrī could ever be—the corpulent *yakṣa* Sarvānubhūti.

Mention must also be made of Kṣetrapāla Bhairava and Hanumān; both beings have similarities with the *yakṣas*—Kṣetrapāla with the maleficent and Hanumān with the beneficent ones—and must therefore be grouped with those supernatural beings. However, the monkey god, like Gomaṭa, has already been denominated "Kāmadeva" though it is difficult to see why: "Kāmadevas" are a subdivision of "Great non-ascetic souls", which certainly does not apply to Gomaṭa, and Hanumān's monkey-looks do not easily entitle him to be considered a "Cupid", if that is what Kāmadeva is supposed to mean. I shall now pass on to describe the iconography of each of these beings in turn.

1 *Sarasvatī*[1]

Sarasvatī is the deified speech of the tīrthaṅkaras, and presides over their teaching. She is also the messenger (*śāsana-*

1. U. P. Shah, "Iconography of the Jain Goddess Sarasvatī", *Journal of the University of Bombay*, X-2 (Sep. 1941), pp. 195-218.

devatā) of the tīrthaṅkaras. The Digambara and Śvetāmbara sects, in their early periods, had a common tradition in representing this goddess, whom they gave a book and a lotus to hold. Afterwards, she began to have a different vehicle in each sect: for the Śvetāmbaras it was a goose and for the Digambaras a peacock. Even so, she is sometimes made to sit on a lotus. (See fig. 2, p. 176.)

Of her symbols, the book is characteristic, and the statue of the squatting Sarasvatī from Mathura already shows it in the right (her left) hand. The Jain Sarasvatī is virtually the Hindu goddess of the same name, and parallels the Buddhist Vajraśāradā, who holds the same symbols. On the roof of J4 (or 30a) at Ellora, she is shown with a figure that looks like Padmāvatī's at Deogarh and Khajuraho, she appears with the *yakṣīs* Padmāvatī and Cakreśvarī; indeed, she herself is sometimes turned into the *yakṣī* of tīrthaṅkaras like Abhinandana and Padmaprabha.

2 *Śrī*

Śrī bathed by elephants is one of the oldest and most popular of Indian art motifs; still I have not been able to find more than one text for it in the Jain iconographical sources, which helps to confirm the thesis that the artists and iconographers were not always interested in the same things. The *śloka* from the *Viṣṇudharmottara* which describes Gajalakṣmī says no more than that the goddess must be on a lotus, hold lotuses in her hands, and be bathed by elephants with pots.

The theme combines objects (and an icon) which in the traditional Indian mind are associated with prosperity, such as the lotus (the most auspicious of flowers), Lakṣmī, "India's brightest goddess" (personification of prosperity) and elephants (symbols of royalty). In early sculpture she is shown with the *yakṣas*[1], guardians of wealth. (See fig. 3, p. 177.)

1. C. Sivaramamurti, "Goddess Lakṣmī and Her Symbols", *Journal of the United Provinces Historical Society* (1941), pp. 21-24.

3 *Saudharmendra*[1]

This god is found in almost every important event of a tīrthaṅkara's life, such as:

a his birth, when the *yakṣa* takes the child on his elephant to Meru for his lustration (*janmābhiṣeka*);[2]

b helps the boy's father to find a wife for his son;[3]

c assists the tīrthaṅkara to carry out any projects for his subjects' welfare;[4]

d prepares for the tīrthaṅkara's coronation and assists in it;[5]

e attends him when he starts for his initiation as a Jain monk;[6]

f takes charge of the *samavasaraṇa* preparations,[7] dances at the end of the discourse,[8] requests the tīrthaṅkara to preach to other beings, and accompanies the procession to the next place of discourse (the dance of Saudharmendra is the only theme represented at Ellora).

g collects the hairs and nails of the tīrthaṅkara after his cremation.[9]

4 *Sarvānubhūti*[10]

Every morning a pious Jain prays to Sarvānubhūti or Sarvāhna, the Jain Kubera related to Jāmbhāla—the Buddhist Kubera. His constant symbols up to the tenth century are a money bag and a citron, but later iconography loads him with a variety of objects and poses.

1. T. N. Ramachandran, *Tiruparuttikunram*, *passim* esp. pp. 65-116.
2. *Ibid.*, p. 65.
3. *Ibid.*, p. 87.
4. *Ibid.*, p. 89.
5. *Ibid.*, pp. 91-92.
6. *Ibid.*, pp. 95-101.
7. *Ibid.*, p. 104.
8. *Ibid.*, p. 111.
9. *Ibid.*, p. 116.
10. *Snātasyāḥ stutiḥ* on Sarvānubhūti :

निष्पङ्कव्योमनीलद्युतिमलसदृशं बालचन्द्राभदंष्ट्रं
मत्तं घण्टारवेन प्रसृतमदजलं पूरयन्तं समन्तात् ।

His pose[1] when sitting, has his right leg down and the left tucked up on the seat. The Digambaras give him three heads and at least six weapons—the *śakti*, a flower, the *abhaya* pose, the *kaṭaka* pose, an axe and a rod. His cognizance is a small temple. The Ellora Sarvānubhūti does not honour these prescriptions, and is nearer to the later Śvetāmbara formulae for the *yakṣa*. These specify sometimes one, and sometimes three heads; 4 or 6 arms, with objects and poses which are no less than 14—*abhaya*, elephant goad, *varada*, noose, whip, hammer, club, fruit, staff, axe, discus, mongoose, trident and spear. The fruit corresponds to the citron of the known sculptures, and the mongoose to the purse (for that animal's skin was often used to make purses out of). The vehicle of this *yakṣa* is either a man or an elephant.

As in the case of other *yakṣas*, the objects and attributes of Sarvānubhūti are had in common with others; in this case it is Mātaṅga, who according to the Digambaras has four arms—the upper two raised in worship and touching his crown. According to the Śvetāmbaras he has only two—holding the citron and the mongoose. In both cases he rides on an elephant. Here again our Ellora figures correspond to the Śvetāmbara description.

5 *Gomukha*[2]

There is only one important sculpture of this *yakṣa* in the Ellora caves, and that is of the Yādava period. It agrees fully with the Digambara specifications; head of cow or ox; four arms with axe, pomegranate, *abhaya* and rosary; bull as vehicle.

आरूढो दिव्यनागं विचरति गगने कामदः कामरूपी
यक्षः सर्वानुभूतिर्दिशतु मम सदा सर्वकार्येषु सिद्धिम् ॥

quoted by U. P. Shah in "Female Chauri-bearer from Ankoṭṭaka and the school of the Ancient West", *Bulletin of the Prince of Wales Museum of Western India*, no. 1 (1950-1951), p. 46. See also *Ibid.*, pp. 45-46.

1. T. N. Ramachandran, *op. cit.*, pp. 208-209.

2. *Ibid.*, p. 197. The Pudukottai bronze of Ṛṣabha, which U. P. Shah dates to c. A. D. 1000, shows the *yakṣa* Gomukha as attendant. See T. S. Sundaran, "Jain Bronzes from Pudukottai", *Lalit Kalā*, nos. 1-2 (April 1955-March 1956), fig. 2.

The Śvetāmbara gives him four arms and a choice of five objects and poses—rosary, *varada*, citron, noose and axe. His vehicle can be either a bull or (incongruously) an elephant. (See fig. 4, p. 178.)

6 *Ambikā*[1]

Ambikā is the most popular of the Jain *yakṣīs*; she is an equivalent of the Hindu Durgā, and like her rides on a lion. The story of how an ordinary woman became Ambikā has Digambara and Śvetāmbara variants, and the former, closely adhered to by the Ellora sculptors, is as follows :[2]

In a city called Girinagara, a brahmin called Somaśarman lived with his wife, Agnilā. They had two sons, Śubāṅkara, aged seven, and Prabhāṅkara, five. One day he invited some brahmins to a funeral ceremony (*śrāddha*) in honour of his ancestors, and when the time came to make the piṇḍa offerings, they went to a nearby tank, leaving Agnilā behind with the cooking. When she was alone, she heard a Jain monk, Varadatta, call on the outside and ask for some food with which to break his month-long fast. Agnilā fed him from the dishes cooked for the brahmins, thus polluting it for their use. Not long after Varadatta had left the brahmins came back and were furious. Somaśarman, furious, drove Agnilā from the house and the poor woman, with her boys, could not think of anywhere else to go but to Varadatta's penance spot. But the ascetic would have none of her. Disconsolate, Agnilā went further up the hill, not knowing what to do. But she had not reckoned with the power of her virtue and chastity, for when she sat down under a tree, it became a wishing tree, giving her all she needed. A dry tank nearby always over-flowed with water whenever she went near it.

The gods were angry at the treatment of Agnilā and burned Girinagara to the ground—except her husband's house. So everybody said that it was the wife's saintliness that had saved

1. U. P. Shah, "Iconography of the Jain Goddess Ambikā", *Journal of the University of Bombay*, IX-2 (Sep. 1940), pp. 147-169.

2. T. N. Ramachandran, *op. cit.*, pp. 157-159.

the building. The brahmins now begged to be allowed to eat the same food which they had earlier spurned as impure.

Stricken with remorse, Somaśarman decided that the least he could do was to find his wife and beg for her forgiveness. Agnilā, from afar on her hill, saw her husband coming, and thinking that it was to punish her further, jumped into a precipice and died. She was reborn the next instant as Ambikā. Almost at once she went back to her sons, and, so as not to frighten them, resumed her previous form.

In the meantime, Somaśarman arrived on the spot and entreated her whom he thought was his wife to forgive him. The woman then took on her *yakṣī* form, and the brahmin fainted at the sight. Coming to his senses he realized that his wife was dead, and in grief jumped into the same precipice, was killed by the fall and almost instantaneously reborn as a lion. The beast came to where Ambikā was, licked her feet, and became her vehicle. The sons were later initiated by Neminātha, whose *yakṣī* the mother ultimately became.

7 *Cakreśvarī*

In later iconography[1] this *yakṣī* becomes the attendant of Ṛṣabha. Her left leg usually hangs down, and her right one is tucked up. Common factors between the iconography of the two sects are that she holds a disk and rides Garuḍa[2]. Digambara specifications are that she has sixteen arms—*abhaya*, *kaṭaka* two on her lap, and eight with various weapons.

The Śvetāmbaras also call her Apraticakrā and say that she ought to have eight or twelve arms—with *varada*, arrow, discus, noose, elephant's goad, bow, thunderbolt, *śakti*, lotus and citron as objects and poses to choose from. She can have three eyes in her head.

1. See B. C. Bhattacarya, *Indian Images II. Jaina Iconography*, Lahore, 1939, ch. 3, p. 121, where he quotes Vasunandi's *Pratiṣṭhāsārasaṅgraha* and *Pratiṣṭhāsāroddhāra*. See also images in the Lucknow Museum 8-9/499 and those at the Deogarh Fort. *Annual Reports of the Archaeological Department* 1917-1918, pl. 2.

2. Bhattacarya, *op. cit.*, p. 121.

8 *Padmāvatī*

According to some iconographical[1] texts this *yakṣī*, wife of Dharaṇendra (who saved Pārśva during his harassment by Meghamālin), can have either four, six, eight or twenty-four arms. When she has four, they hold a goad, a rosary and two lotuses; when she has six, they have a noose, a spear, a sword, a crescent, a club and a staff; when eight-handed, she is given the noose and "other (unspecified) attributes". When twenty-four-handed these are her attributes—conch, sword, disk, crescent, lotus, blue lotus, bow, *śakti*, noose, *kuśa* grass, bell, arrow, staff, shield, trident, axe, thunderbolt, garland, fruit, club, leaf, stalk, *varada* and another object which the iconographer forgot to mention.

The specifically Digambara text lays down that she should have four arms, with two of her hands holding each an axe and a thunderbolt, and the other two in *abhaya* and *kaṭaka*. She has to have a five-hooded snake hovering over her crown, with the goose as her cognizance. The Śvetāmbaras also prescribe four arms, with a fruit, a goad, a lotus and a noose, with a cock-serpent (*kukkuṭasarpa*) as her vehicle—which is sometimes specified by the Digambara text too.[2]

9 *Kṣetrapāla*

There are five types of *kṣetrapālas*[3] or field guardians :

1 Maṇibhadra
2 Bhairava
3 Vīrabhadra
4 Jaya
5 Vijaya

Our *kṣetrapāla* is obviously the second of these. His shrine is placed on the outskirts of a town to protect it against evil deities and men. This god, popular with the iconographers,

1. *Pratiṣṭhāsārasaṅgraha*, quoted by ibid., *op. cit.*, ch. 3, p. 144, footnote 2.

2. See also Malliṣeṇa, *Bhairava-Padmāvatī Kalpa*.

3. See also Āśādhara, *Pūjāpāṭha* and the *Kṣetrapālapūjā* (5 types of Kṣetrapālas).

appears only in the Yādava sculptures at Ellora. The information we get on him, when we put the texts together, is as follows :[1]

a. Number of arms : 2, 4, 6, 8 and 20.

b. Objects held in hands, and hand poses: trident, skull, club, *kheṭaka*, snake, *tomara*, drum, *khaṭvāṅga*, sword, bell, noose, fire, *ṭaṅka*, *abhaya*, *varada*, bow, arrow, *mudgara*, dog, goad and *geḍika*.

c. Facial details : three eyes, tusks (sharp or curved) stiff hair (sometimes red), "barbarian" (*barbara*) hair, matted hair.

d. Details of torso : nude, with a snake (sometimes Vāsuki) for sacred thread, garland of snakes (*takṣakas*), garland of heads, snake ornaments and lion skin covering.

e. Details of feet : wearing wooden sandals.

f. Seat : a dead body.

g. Vehicle : a dog. (See fig. 5, P. 179)

10 *Hanumān*

This monkey god is the devotee and friend of Rāma, who helped him to fight the *rākṣasas*. He is mentioned in one text[2] together with Kṣetrapāla and Vaṭuka Bhairava. In the Yādava sculptures he is once placed alongside *kṣetrapāla*. If we ask why Hanumān appears in a Jain temple, we can be given at least three reasons. First, the popularity of the monkey god in the Maratha country, in which Ellora has long been situated; besides, the Yādavas themselves were a Marathi-speaking dynasty. For the Marathas, Hanumān is almost a second Gaṇeśa, the remover of obstacles (*vighnahara*). However, an icon popular with one religion cannot be taken over by another without it

1. See the *Ācāradinakara*, *Nirvāṇakalikā*, *Suprabhedāgama*, *Kṣetrapālapūjā* quoted by Bhattacharya, *op. cit.*, ch. 7, pp. 180-181.

2. The *Ācāradinakara* couples the names of Hanumān (and the other gods) with that of Kṣetrapāla :

वटुकनाथहनुमान्नरसिंहादिपुरपूजिदेशपूजितप्रतिष्ठा ।

Quoted by Bhattacarya, *op, cit.*, p. 181.

being made to fit in with the latter's categories. This brings us to our second reason: Hanumān was already long a Jain figure because of his unavoidable inclusion in the Rāmāyaṇa, of which the Jains had their own version. The third reason is that he became a sort of honorary *yakṣa*. He has the qualities of one—he can fly through the air, assume any shape at will, is of immense strength, and is often worshipped in connexion with trees. We must remember that the *yakṣas* in course of time came to be called *vīras*, and Hanumān has always been known as Mahāvīra. In the Uttar Pradesh *yakṣarātri* (or Dīvāli) is said to be his birthday, and he is supposed to like perfumes, flowers and red lead coatings for his images, which are other characteristics of the *yakṣas*.[1]

V HUMAN ACTIVITIES

While the superhuman beings inhabit the two extreme ends of the Jain universe, the human and animal ones are found in the middle world. Most human beings do not know even the word *dharma*. They are the *mlecchas*, or barbarians. The Aryas know the word, but not all are aware of what it implies, as many of them have "teachers of limited knowledge, who consider themselves omniscient, describe the state of liberation in utterly different ways, with words of fallacious reasoning which do not touch its nature". The only ship capable of crossing the sea of *saṁsāra* is the doctrine of the Jinas, and has the tīrthaṅkaras for its boatmen.[2]

1. Moti Chandra, "Some Aspects of Yakṣa Cult in Ancient India", *Bulletin of the Prince of Wales Museum of Western India*, no. 3 (1952-1953), pp. 61-62.

2. उद्दीप्ताखिलरत्नमुद्धृतजडं नानानयान्तर्गृहं
सस्यात्कारसुधाभिलिप्ति जनिभृत्कारुण्यकूपोच्छ्रितम् ।
आरोप्य श्रुतयानपात्रममृतद्वीपं नयन्तः परा-
नेते तीर्थंकृतो मदीयहृदये मध्येभवाब्ध्यासताम् ॥

"May they dwell in my heart—the Tīrthakaras who, taking on board the ship of sacred lore—possessed of all brilliant jewels, freed from bilge-water (*otherwise* saving the ignorant), containing cabins of various models of argument, painted with the lime (or nectar) of the *syātkāra*, and furnished with the high mast of compassion for living creatures —others (found)

Yet, not even the Jains are all equally perfect. Some wish to renounce all sin like the monk, as well as attachment to home and possessions. Others cannot desist from every sin, or separate themselves from family and business. These are the householders. The monk thus takes the major vows and the householder the minor ones: to abstain completely or partially from injury, falsehood, stealing, unchastity and attachment.[1]

1 WAR : *THE RESCUE OF PRASENAJIT*

With all their hatred for injury, the Jains still lavished praise on their warriors, historical or mythical. Among the latter were the twelve world emperors or *cakravartins*, the first of whom was Bharata, defeated in contest by his brother Bāhubali. Three of the tīrthaṅkaras were themselves *cakravartins* before enlightenment—Śāntinātha, Kunthunātha and Aranātha. The last but one tīrthaṅkara, Pārśvanātha, was himself a warrior, as can be seen from the episode of his encounter with Yavana. There is a battle scene in a panel at Ellora near the Indra Sabhā (between J 10 and J 14), beneath the figures of the meditating tīrthaṅkara and a scripture-stand, which most probably represents this event.

Hemacandra's[2] account, however, excludes any real fighting, and is as follows. A king of a city named Kuśasthala, called Prasenajit, had a daughter Prabhāvatī, for whom he could find no worthy groom, except only Pārśva. When king Yavana found this out, he came in force to Kuśasthali and laid siege to it, hoping that this would make Prasenajit give him his daughter. However, a messenger managed to slip out of the besieged city at night and went to Pārśva's father to ask for help, but it was Pārśva himself who took charge of the counter-attacking army.

in the middle of the ocean of worldly existence, carry them over to the island of immortality."

Śravaṇa Belgola Inscription no. 258 (108) in Siddhara Basti, dated A.D. 1432. *Epigraphia Carnatica*, Vol. II. Text p. 128, translation, p. 116.

1. *Sarvārthasiddhi*, ch. VII, *Reality*, pp. 189-191.
2. Hemacandra, *op. cit.*, vol. 5, pp. 385-391.

But no fighting ensued. When Pārśva's messenger upbraided Yavana for his foolishness for now taking arms against the "lord of the world", and when a minister sided with the messenger, the irate king's pride was humbled; then, tying an axe round his neck, he went into Pārśva's presence imploring forgiveness. Not very long afterwards Pārśva decided to dedicate himself entirely to religion.

2 *RELIGIOUS ACTIVITIES*

Perhaps the best visual summing up of Jain religious activity is the iconographical type of later ages called the *siddhacakra*,[1] which is a diagram of the "Nine Dignities" (*navapada*) of Jainism. The first five of these are the Pañcaparameṣṭins or the "Five Supreme Ones". The two sects disagree in describing the remaining four. The Śvetāmbaras say that they are Right Knowledge, Right Belief, Right Conduct, and Right Penance. The Digambaras are more concrete, and visualize them as the Jina image, the Jina temple, the Wheel of Law and the Jain Scriptures.

Many of these categories have already been studied. As to the Pañcaparameṣṭins, we have dealt with the Siddha and the Arhat. Of the last 4 *padas*, the Jina image is in a sense the subject of this book, and the Wheel of Law is no more than a decorative detail on the tīrthaṅkaras' throne bases. What remains to be examined are the Upādhyāya, Ācārya and Sādhu of the Parameṣṭins, and the Jina temple and the Jain scriptures of the four last *padas*. The layman is an integral part of this picture, because he is the prop of the ascetic's way of life and hence of the *mokṣamārga*.[2] Thus the entire circle of Jain religious practices is comprehended in the *siddhacakra* symbol.

1. U. P. Shah, *Studies in Jaina Art*, pp. 97-103.
2. मोक्षस्य कारणमभिष्टुतमत्र लोके
    तद्धार्यते मुनिभिरङ्गबलात्तदन्नात् ॥
   तद्दीयते च गृहिणा गुरुभक्तिभाजा
    तस्माद्धृतो गृहजनेन विमुक्तिमार्गः ॥

   Padmānandi, *Pañcaviṁśati*, 2, 12.

The Jain texts lay down laws for both ascetic and layman to practise their type of vow. The ascetic is helped to carry out his vow by four accessories[1] a scripture stand (*sthāpanācārya*), a mouth piece (*mukhapaṭṭikā*), a broom (*daṇḍaproñcānaka*) and a rosary (*japamālikā*), the last of which can be used by a layman too. I shall now describe these briefly in turn:

1 The *scripture stand* or *sthāpanā* (*sthāpanācārya*)[2] which is more than just a stand on which to rest the scriptures. It is also a symbolic installation of the absent *ācārya*, and is meant to remind the Jain monk, engaged in giving a discourse, of his teacher. It is a mark of reverence to the latter, a symbol of his presence, and a sort of corrective witness, discouraging scriptural misinterpretation.[3]

Two pieces of wood are crossed and tied at the crossing with a string. When opened out they form a stand, on top of which a fine piece of cloth, often richly embroidered, is put as a cover. The crossing arms of the stand are often made of ivory and sandalwood, with decorative carvings.

2 The *mask* or *mouthpiece* (*mukhapaṭṭikā*),[4] which both prevents insects entering the mouth (and getting killed) and symbolizes speech control. When not used it is often held in the hand, and has a shape which in sculptures leads one to mistake it for the leaf of a sacred text.

A. N. Upadhye & H. L. Jain (Ed.), Padmānandi's *Pañcaviṁśati* (Jivarāja Jaina Granthamālā, No. 10), Sholapur: Jaina Saṁskṛti Saṁrakshaka Saṅgha, 1962.

1. "...the Anuyogadvāracūrṇi...mentions the accessories for a sādhu in the practice of dharma; they are...sthāpanā...mukhapaṭṭikā... daṇḍa-proñchānaka...japamālikā". U. P. Shah, *op. cit.*, p. 114.

2. *Ibid.*, pp. 113-114, mentions and quotes the following authorities: Bhadrabāhu, *Piṇḍaniryukti*, pp. 3-7 with Malayagiri's commentary; and Jinabhadra Kṣamaṇāśrama, *Viśeṣāvaśyaka Mahābhāṣya.*

3. *Ibid.*, p. 113.

4. *Ibid.*, pp. 114-115 mentions and quotes the following texts: Yatidinācārya, *Pañcavastuprakaraṇa*; the *Oghaniryuktivṛtti*; the *Bṛhatkalpabhāṣya*, vol. 4, v. 3982; *Piṇḍaniryukti*, with the commentary of Malayagiri, p. 13.

3 The *broom* (*daṇḍaproñcānaka* or *rajoharaṇa*).[1] Unlike the usual Indian article, this is a broom with a handle, used to sweep dust particles and small insects from one's path. Among the materials employed are wool, camel hair, jute, *valkala* fibres, *muñja* grass and peacock feathers.

4 *Rosary beads* (*japamālikā*),[2] made of conch, sandal, coral, crystal, gems, gold or silver.

These accessories help the three types of ascetics and the layman to follow four of Jainism's important principles: compassion, charity, asceticism and knowledge. The essence of *dharma* is compassion[3]—without it the other principles are of little use—and two of the four accessories, the mask and the broom, aid the three ascetics in achieving this. The teaching of the scriptures and the imparting of religious knowledge presumably distinguish the Ācarya and Upādhyāya from the Sādhu; here the scripture stand is a useful accessory. The rosary aids both ascetic and layman in *dhyāna*.

As I said before, the layman is the support of the ascetic, and one of his main tasks is charity, to support the ascetics and others. The houses of those householders who do not give to ascetics are real nooses of bondage. Here, as in other religions, the tasks of the layman (as a bishop remarked in a session of the second Vatican Council), are to believe, pray, obey and pay. (See fig. 6, P. 180).

To sum up. Of the Nine Dignities, the Tīrthaṅkara and the Arhat constitute the top level, and include the Jina image and the Wheel of Law. A second level of the Dignities, formed by the three unenlightened ascetics and the layman, are related to the accessories of the monk, the almsgiving of the layman and the Jain temple. There are two reliefs carved face to face in the Indra Sabhā:[4] one represents the five Parameṣ-

1. *Ibid.*, quotes *Piṇḍaniryukti*, *loc. cit.*
2. *Ibid.* p. 115.
3. Padmānandi, *op. cit.*, I : v. 7.
4. See Jain Caves J 18-(1), (14).

ṭins and the other the Jain temple,[1] both together thus being a summing up of Jainism.

1. THE JAIN TEMPLE

श्रीकान्ताकुलवेश्म किं वरयशः कान्ताप्रमोदागरं
भूकान्तारतिसद्म सज्जयवधूक्रीडास्पदं किं पुनः ।
स्यात्कारोज्ज्वलसन्नयद्वयममी श्रीभारतीरङ्गभूः
स्वःश्रीमुक्तिरमास्वयंवरगृहं श्रीजैनगेहं वृणे ॥ ७ ॥

"Is this the noble abode of the lady Śrī? The excellent pleasure house of the lady Fame? The house of amorous enjoyment of the lady Earth? Again, is this the sporting place of the virtuous woman Victory? (This) prosperous Jain abode (is indeed) the stage consisting of the two excellent doctrines resplendent with the word *syāt*, (whereupon) the glorious Bhāratī (dances), the house where (the ladies) Heavenly Bliss, Salvation and Prosperity choose their husbands." Karkala Inscription of Bhairava II, (March 1856), *Epigraphia Indica* Vol. VIII, p. 132.

Chapter IV

A CONSPECTUS OF THE ELEMENTS OF ELLORA JAIN ICONOGRAPHY

Nam omnium magnarum artium sicut arborum altitudo nos delectat, radices stirpesque non item.

Cicero, *Orator* xliii, 147.

In the great arts, as in great trees, it is the height that delights us, not the roots and the stems

Nothing in the study of art history is calculated to cause tedium more than iconographical analyses—except of course to those who are addicted to that kind of thing—and nothing is more arduous than to attempt to dissolve the sand of iconographical minutiae into the stream of running prose. Not everything in a sentence can receive equal emphasis; the dull details of iconography make the attention to wander constantly; a trivial item may be needed afterwards for reference : hence the only practical way of presenting iconographical details seems to be catalogue-wise, with the particulars distributed under broad headings.

In arranging my matter I have followed a numerical classification—not the decimal one, for it is a nuisance to have constantly to put the dots between the figures—but what we may call a system of two integers, the first two of which stand for the broad categories (in our case totalling 55), with the integers that follow representing the subdivisions. Thus the integers that constitute 14 signify TREE; 142, the second subdivision of 14, for VARIETIES of TREE; 1422, the second subdivision of 142, for BANYAN tree. An 0 that follows the second or subsequent integers negates that which precedes it; thus 122 stands for KNOBS, and 1220 for NO KNOBS, that is, absence of knobs in a place where knobs are frequent.

This numbering will be of use in the future for the accurate description of the icons of the Ellora Jain caves, and indeed of all images whose iconography is as dreary and redundant as ours. For instance, instead of writing out a description, such as the one which follows, hundreds of times, it would be more economical to indicate it by numbers (shown in brackets, the meaning of which is explained below) : Tīrthaṅkara in panel (011), with locks on shoulders (023), an ovaloid halo (0311), seated on a lotus (085) placed on a throne which has three compartments, one occupied by a wheel and the other two by a lion each (1012), the tīrthaṅkara having behind him a cushion with flower-shaped embroidered bosses (1121)—and so on. This method would enable the researcher to find out which combinations of the numbered elements are more frequent, and which less, much as the translations of logical concepts into the symbols of mathematical logic lead the philosopher to discover the character and frequency of the patterns of human thought.

But such classifications are necessarily imperfect. Logical exactitude demands a clear division of categories; but reality is richer than logic, and the same object can be subsumed under more than one class; for instance, the eagle or *garuḍa* (5562) is not only a bird, but can also be a goddess's base (08). In such cases, it is advisable to give the equivalence in brackets (08=5562).

The richness of reality (which is multidimensional) also makes it hard for logic (which is linear) to fully grasp it, hence classifications can never tell us all about our subject, especially about those aspects of it which are not clear to us. I have thus only tried to classify the fixed types of Jain iconography, and have had to leave out types such as unidentified goddesses with identifiable symbols :

01 FRAME

- 011 Panel
- 012 Arch
- 013 Niche
- 014 Pavilion (*maṇḍapa*)

02 BODY ATTRIBUTES

- 021 *Uṣṇīṣa*
- 022 Hair on head
- 023 Locks on shoulder
- 024 *Śrīvatsa*

03 POSTURE

- 031 Sitting
  - 0311 Symmetrical
    - 03111 *vīrāsana*
    - 03112 *padmāsana*
  - 0312 Asymmetrical
    - 03121 One leg tucked up
- 032 Standing
  - 0321 Symmetrical
    - *Kāyotsarga*
  - 0322 Flexional
  - 0323 Irregular

04 HALO

- 041 Shape
  - 0411 Ovaloid
  - 0412 Ovaloid joined to rectangular
- 042 Forms of top of halo
  - 0421 Round
  - 0422 Pointed
  - 0423 Twisted
  - 0424 With design
- 043 Form of ends of halo
  - 0431 Plain
  - 0432 Scrolled
- 044 *Makara*
  - 0441 Plain
  - 0442 Foliated
  - 0443 Boy on *makara*
  - 0444 Boy behind *makara*
- 045 Surface
  - 0451 Plain
  - 0452 Jewelled
  - 0453 Jewel-garlanded
  - 0454 Broad curved and ornamented
  - 0455 Incised rim
- 046 Border beyond rim
  - 0461 Plain

- 0462 Flaming
- 0463 Lotus-petalled

05 ANIMAL FORMS AND SYMBOLS

- 051 Snake hoods (Pārśvanātha)
  - 0511 Five hoods
  - 0512 Seven hoods
- 052 Snake body convolutions (Pārśvanātha)
  - 0521 Left side
  - 0522 Right side
  - 0523 Snake tail
- 053 Bull (Ṛṣabha)

06 PLANT FORMS AND SYMBOLS

- 061 Twists between legs
- 062 Curves on body
- 063 Curves on sides of arms
- 064 Curves on each side of legs
- 065 Creeper, not Gomaṭa's

07 OBJECTS NEAR TĪRTHAṄKARAS

- 071 Chowries
- 072 Jars
- 073 Clouds

08 BASE

- 081 Plain
- 082 Board
- 083 Pedestal
- 084 Anthill
- 085 Lotus
- 086 Cushion
- 087 Foot rest
- 088 Lotus foot rest

09 SEAT

- 091 Cushion
- 092 Lotus with stalk
- 093 Cloth

10 THRONE BASE

101 Compartments
- 1011 Wheel
- 1012 Wheel and lions
- 1013 Wheel, lions and elephants
- 1014 Lions
- 1015 Lions and elephants
- 1016 Figure with wheel
- 1017 Winged figure and lion
- 1018 *Navagrahas*, the nine planets

102 Shape of base face
- 1021 Unbroken
- 1022 Modulated

11 THRONE CUSHION

111 Shape
- 1111 Ovaloid
- 1112 Rectangular with fluffy ends

112 Embossed trimming on the sides
- 1121 Flower-shaped
- 1122 Nipple-shaped

12 THRONE BACK

121 Plain back
122 Beam end
123 *Makara*
124 Rampant *yālis*

13 UMBRELLA

131 Tiers
- 1311 One-tier
- 1312 Two-tier
- 1313 Three-tier

132 Knobs
- 1320 No knobs
- 1321 One knob
- 1322 Two knobs

14 TREE

141 Parts
- 1411 Trunk
- 1412 Branches
- 1413 Tendrils
- 1414 Leaves
- 1415 Flowers
- 1416 Fruit

142 Varieties
- 1421 Aśoka
- 1422 Banyan
- 1423 Mango or mango-jackfruit
- 1424 Stylized

15 MALE THRONE ATTENDANTS

151 Number
- 1511 Two
- 1512 Four

152 Position
- 1521 In relation to the throne
- 1522 In relation to the beholder
- 1523 Visibility

153 Head
- 1531 Height
- 1532 Headgear

154 Halo

155 Hands
- 1551 Object holding
- 1552 Free
- 1553 Poses

156 Elbows
- 1561 Non-resting
- 1562 Resting

157 Sacred thread

158 Waist band

16 FEMALE THRONE ATTENDANTS

(Particulars as in 14)

161 Number

162 Position
163 Head
164 Halo
165 Hands
166 Elbows

17 DRUMMERS
171 Drums and hands
172 Only drums

18 CYMBALISTS
181 Cymbals and hand
182 Only cymbals

19 CONCH-BLOWERS

20 TRUMPETEERS

21 FLAUTISTS

22 BELL RINGER

23 MUSICIANS WITH OTHER INSTRUMENTS
231 *viṇā* player
232 Musicians with unidentifiable instruments

24 GARLAND-BEARERS

25 LOTUS-HOLDERS
251 Male
252 Female

26 FLOWER-HOLDERS
261 Male
262 Female

27 OBJECT-HOLDERS
271 Male
272 Female

28 FLOWER-THROWERS
281 Male
282 Female

29 FREE FIGURES
291 Male
292 Female

30 TEACHING ĀCĀRYA (UPĀDHYĀYA)
301 Hand poses
3011 Teaching
3012 Holding sacred text (*or mukhapaṭṭikā* ?)

31 DEVOTEES
- 311 Ordinary
  - 3111 Male
  - 3112 Female
- 312 Special
  - 3121 Male
  - 3122 Female

32 *GAṆAS*

33 ASCETICS

34 FIGHTERS (IN PĀRŚVANĀTHA'S TEMPTATION)
- 341 Weapon holders
  - 3411 Dagger
  - 3412 Sword
  - 3413 Trident
  - 3414 Club
  - 3415 Mace
  - 3416 Spear
  - 3417 Bow and arrow
  - 3418 Shield
- 342 Elephant-goad holders
- 343 Snake holders
- 344 Rock throwers
  - 3441 Stone throwers
  - 3442 Rock hurlers
- 345 Apparel
  - 3451 Sacred thread
  - 3452 Serpent necklace
  - 3453 Short dhoti
  - 3454 Armlet
  - 3455 Double anklet
  - 3456 Large earrings

35 TERRIFIERS AND MONSTERS (IN PĀRŚVANĀTHA'S TEMPTATION)
- 351 Monster face
- 352 Demon belly
- 353 Flying *gaṇa*
- 354 Female fiend
- 355 Lion-headed monster carrying fiend

356 Large tusks
357 Large penis

36 ANIMAL RIDERS (based on 55, *q.v.*; deduct 55 and Join remaining digits to 36)

3611 On buffalo
3612 Deer
3615 Elephant
3617 Ram
3622 Lion
3623 Tiger
3651 Goose

37 CREEPER HOLDERS (IN HOMAGE TO BĀHUBALI)

371 Hand poses

3711 Inner hands raised to shoulder, outer hands hanging
3712 Inner hands raised to shoulder, outer hands turned inwards
3713 Irregular poses

372 Halo

38 SNAKE FIGURES

381 *Nāginīs*, with hoods and tale
382 With hoods only

39 DHARAṆENDRA AND WOMAN (IN PĀRŚVANĀTHA'S TEMPTATION)

40 MEGHAMĀLIN AND WOMAN (IN PĀRŚVANĀTHA'S TEMPTATION)

41 SAUDHARMENDRA

42 SARVĀNUBHŪTI

421 Objects and poses

4211 Pomegranate
4212 Purse

422 Headgear

4221 *kirīṭa*
4222 *karaṇḍa*

43 GOMUKHA

431 Objects and poses

4311 Rosary

4312 Citron
4313 Axe
4314 *Varada*
432 Headgear
44 ŚAṄKHANIDHI
441 Objects and poses
4411 Conch
442 Headgear
45 PADMANIDHI
451 Objects and poses
4511 Lotus
452 Headgear
46 BRAHMA YAKṢA ?
461 Objects and poses
462 Headgear
47 AMBIKĀ
471 Objects
4711 Mangoes
4712 Noose
4713 Food
472 Headgear
473 Foot ornaments
474 Children
4741 Elder
4742 Younger
475 Husband
48 CAKREŚVARĪ
481 Objects
4811 Lotus bud, or flower
4812 Disk
4813 Conch
4814 Sword
4815 Club
4816 Rod
4817 Elephant goad
4818 Bow
4819 *vajra* thunderbolt

49 KṢETRAPĀLA
491 Number of arms
4911 Two
4912 Four
492 Objects and poses
4921 Drum
4922 Club
4923 Dagger
4924 *abhaya*
493 Dog
4931 Barking
4932 On leash

50 HANUMĀN
501 Objects and poses
5011 Dagger in waist
502 Feet
5021 On cowering figure
5022 On ground

51 GAJALAKṢMĪ OR ŚRĪ
511 Number of elephants
5111 Two
5112 Four
512 Lotus pond

52 SARASVATĪ OR PRAJÑAPTIDEVĪ
521 Objects and poses
5211 *varada* ?
5212 Lotus on stalk ?
5213 Palm-leaf book ?
5214 *śakti* ?

53 APRATICAKRĀ
531 Objects and poses

54 PADMĀVATĪ
541 Objects and poses
5411 Noose
5412 *varada*
5413 Fruit ?

55 FAUNA

- 551 Herbivorous mammals
  - 5511 Buffalo
  - 5512 Bull
  - 5513 Cow/calf
  - 5514 Deer
  - 5515 Elephant
  - 5516 Horse ?
  - 5517 Ram
  - 5518 Squirrel
- 552 Carnivorous mammals
  - 5521 Dog ?
  - 5522 Lion
  - 5523 Tiger ?
  - 5524 *yāli*
- 553 Reptiles
  - 5531 Crocodile or *makara*
  - 5532 Snake
  - 5533 *kukkuṭa-sarpa* "cockserpent"
- 554 Rodents
  - 5541 Mouse
- 555 Insects
  - 5551 Scorpion
- 556 Birds
  - 5561 Ducks or geese
  - 5562 Eagle or *garuḍa*
  - 5563 Parrot
  - 5564 Peacock

56 JAIN OBJECTS OF WORSHIP

- 561 *jinālaya*, Jain temple
- 562 *sthāpanācārya*, scripture stand

Appendix I

THE INSCRIPTIONS AT ELLORA[1]

The temples at Ellora have at least 15 inscriptions :

1	A.D. 500-600	Cave 19
2	600-800	Râmeshvara (cave 21)
3	700-750	Dashâvatâra (cave 15)
4	700-800	Kailâsa 1
5	700-800	Kailâsa 2
6	700-900	Vishvakarma (cave 10)
7	750-850	Jain caves (Kannada inscriptions)
8	800-1000	Jain caves (Sanskrit inscriptions)
9	890-900	Kailâsa 3
10	1150 ?	Kailâsa 4
11	1150 ?	Kailâsa 5
12	1234-1235	Pārśvanātha-on-the-hill
13	1329	Kailâsa 6
14	1390	Kailâsa 7
15	1462	Kailâsa 8

Though nos. 2, 5, 8, 9, 10, 12, 14 and 15 are irrelevant to our study, I shall, for completeness sake, examine all the inscriptions in order.

1 CAVE 19. At the foot of the Lakulīśa panel in the centre of the shrine door lintel : unpublished.[2]

2 RĀMESHVARA : श्री नागदेव "the name of some visitor from the south, in characters of the 7th or 8th century".[3]

3 DASHĀVATĀRA : Verse 29, lines 13 and 14.

1. The material of this appendix is mainly from *Inscriptions of the Cave Temples of Western India*, Miscellaneous Publication of the Archaeological Survey of India, no. 10, pp. 91-100.

2. First noticed by Walter Spink, "Ellora's Earliest Phase", *Bulletin of The American Academy of Benares*, Vol. I, Nov. 1967, p. 13, footnote 9.

3. *Inscriptions of the Cave Temples of Western India*, p. 98.

यस्याखण्डितविक्रमस्य कटकेनाक्रम्य तीरक्षिर्ति
सौघेऽस्मिन्कृतगुर्जरेन्द्ररुचिरे रम्ये U तैस्तस्थुषः ।
स्नान्तीभिUU ताङ्गरागसुरभि प्रोत्कम्पिपद्माकरं
घारित्रेष्वपि पुष्करेष्वपिU – – – Uनाभिश्चिरम् ॥[1]

The inscription (which on the style of its lettering is said to date between 700 and 750) thus tells us only that he stayed at the temple, and not, as many people assume, that he built it. An earlier verse (n. 23) informs us that by this time he had conquered Vallabha, Sandhubhūpa (or Sandhukūpa), Kāñcī, Kaliṅga, Kosala, Srīśailadeśa, Mālava, Lāṭa and Taṅka. This inscription is thus after 743, the date of Kāñcī's capture. Further examination reveals that by the time of Dashāvatāra inscription Dantidurga was no longer a feudatory, and his liege lord had died in 747. The date of Dantidurga is thus narrowed to the period between 747 and 758 (by which latter date he was either dead or no longer king). As the inscription does not mention the Cālukyas by name, one assumes that he had not yet clashed with the Cālukya Kīrtivarman II which happened before January 754. Considering that he had subdued Maharashtra in 753, it is reasonable to assume that Dantidurga visited Ellora (which is in Maharashtra) just before setting out to attack the Cālukyas that very year.

For us, the Dashāvatāra is an important temple, as it inaugurates the new grand style at Ellora, with its greater emphasis on power, formalism and iconography. In the Jain caves the last two qualities are taken to extreme lengths. We can thus be almost certain that the temple was ready by 753, and certainly by 758.

4 KAILĀSA :

The earliest one of six inscriptions in the temple is to be found on the pilaster to the right of relief of Gajalakṣmī facing the visitor on his entering the court, and under a figure of a four-armed *gaṇa*. Its alphabet belongs to the eighth century and the inscription seems to read like this :—

राढे [कु] लभद्रक्कुरस्य
श्री जलकी [न्दे ?]
दधिचड्ड [ण्ड ?][2]

1. *Ibid.*, p. 95.
2. *Ibid.*, p. 97.

"The 3rd letter is injured and the 7th is read doubtfully-*ṅka*, so also is the last letter of the 2nd line : the last letter legible in the third line may be *dda*, but it is very faint and may be *ṇḍa* or even *dau*. Any interpretation must be doubtful, but it seems probable that the reading is :—

राढेकुल भद्राङ्कुरस्य
श्रीजलक्रीडौ
दधिचण्ड

"(*The gift*) of Lakṣmī sporting in water and Udadhicanda (a *gaṇa* of Śiva), by Bhadrāṅkura of the Rāḍhā family."[1] If this reading is true, it no doubt refers to the Gajalakṣmī of the adjacent panel.

5 KAILĀSA-Inscription 2 : 8th century.

"Beside a *liṅga* on the right of the porch are some four letters in the southern form of alphabet and of about the same age".

It is now opportune to bring in the one loose inscription on the Ellora temples, the Rāṣṭrakūṭa grant of Karka Suvarṇavarṣa, dated *Śaka* 734 (812-813) where we are informed that it was Kṛṣṇa I who commissioned the structure. The relevant verses are the following :

भूयस्तथाविधकृतौ व्यवसायहाने-
रेतन्मया कथमहो कृतमित्यकस्मात् ।
कर्तापि यस्य खलु विस्मयमाप शिल्पी
तन्नाम कीर्तनमकार्यत येन राज्ञा ॥

"[That king] by whom, verily, was caused to be constructed a temple on the hill at Elapura, of a wonderful structure—on seeing which the best of immortals who move in celestial cars, struck with astonishment, think much constantly, saying, 'This temple of Śiva is self-existent; in a thing made by art such beauty is not seen'—a temple the architect-builder of which in consequence of the failure of his energy as regards [the cons-

1.. *Ibid.*

truction of] another such work, was himself suddenly struck with astonishment saying 'Oh, how it was that I built it."[1]

"That king" of course means Kṛṣṇa I :

धर्मात्मनस्तस्य नृपस्य जज्ञे

सुतः सुधर्मा खलु कृष्णराजः ।

"Of that king (Karkarāja), of virtuous disposition, was born a pious son, Krishnarāja".[2]

6 VISHVAKARMA : Letters of the eighth or ninth century :

ये धर्मा हेतुप्रभवा हेतुं तेषां तथागतो ह्यवदत्तेषां च यो निरोध एवंवादी महाश्रमणः[3]

This is the common Buddhist formula, and contains no historical information.

7 JAIN CAVES : This is a Haḷe Kannada inscription, which, as far as I have been able to find out, has never been published. From the form of the alphabet, Fleet ascribes them to about A. D. 750 to 850. Scholars of more recent times are inclined to put it between A.D. 800 and 850.[4] There is another inscription, not (to my knowledge) noticed, in the interior of cave 34 (J 26), on the pillar to the left of the sanctum, below the relief of Pārśvanātha.

8 JAIN CAVES : Two inscriptions in the lower hall of the Indra Sabhā.

(a) "On the front of a square pillar is a colossal figure of a Tīrthaṁkara with a short inscription in the Kāyastha or old Nāgarī character, and attributed by Mr. J. F. Fleet to the 9th or 10th century. It reads :—

श्री नागवर्म्मं क्रिता [कृता] प्रतिमा

'The image was made by Śrī Nāgavarmā."[5]

(b) "At the left or west end of the front aisle is a chapel with colossal Digambara Tīrthaṁkaras on each side of the entrance,

1. R. G. Bhandarkar, "The Rāshṭrakūṭa King Krishnarāja I and Elapura", *Indian Antiquary* XII (1883), pp. 228-229, lines 14-17.

2. *Ibid.*, line 9.

3. *Inscriptions of the Cave Temples*, p. 91.

4. Personal Communication in 1965 from Dr. F. R. Allchin, Lecturer in Indian Studies, University of Cambridge.

5. *Inscriptions of the Cave Temples*, p. 98.

Illustration 5
CAVE 32 (J 13-3) Sohila the ***brahmacārin***, **with inscription.**
C. A. D. 810-880.

[facing p. 91

and under the one on the north or right side is an inscription in three short lines in rather older like characters than the last. It reads :

श्री सोहिल ब्रह्मचारिण: शान्तिभट्टारकप्रतिमेयम् ।

'This is the image of Śāntibhaṭṭāraka (*made by*) Sohila a Brahmacārin"[1] (see Illustration 5).

KAILĀSA—Inscription 3. Ceiling and architrave, (south side). "On the ceiling and architraves of the front porch of the great monolithic temple of Kailāsa there are some remains of painting of three different ages. The lowest of this is perhaps of about the 8th century or when the temple was finished, and done on a ground similar to that used at Ajaṇṭā. An elephant, a human figure, &c., can be distinguished of good execution.

At a later date this has been covered over with a coating of lime and painted upon with figures of the gods, and on the architraves is a battle scene. On the south side are two armies; in the one to the left are a horse and then two elephants; over one are the letters—*luruṁghu* (or *thu* ?), and behind are horseman, &c. The man on the horse has a spear in the arm. To his right is an elephant bearing a spearman, who is about to slay the horseman, and a man is represented falling down. Above the elephant painted in modern Devanāgarī characters, we read—

स्वस्ति श्री परमारिराउ

and over the horseman—

मलगहृ

Behind Parimārirāū's elephants are footmen in mail bearing spears and round shields, their hair tied with a band, and all with a band, and all with large earrings—as the Arab writers remarked of the Rāshṭrakūṭas, behind are horsemen with swords and shields."[2]

Bhagavanlal Indraji doubts as to whether this might be Kṛṣṇadeva Paramāra (reigned from about 890—900), but is not certain that that king came in contact with the Muslims whom he takes the painting to represent.

1. *Inscriptions of the Cave Temples* p. 99.
2. *Ibid.*, p. 96.

9 KAILĀSA — Inscription 4 : Ceiling and architraves (west side) *c.* A. D. 1150 ?

"On the west side, a rājā is represented seated with a *chhatra* held over him; to the left some people are paying respects to him and to the right are two bearded men seated with *chhatras*. Over the rājā is written :-

स्वस्ति कन्नुदेवराय

and over the man

—ररण (or ? ल)

the rest is lost.

This Kannuradeva is probably Kṛishṇadeva or Kannaradeva II of the Nikumbhavaṁśa, who ruled at Patna probably as feudatories of the Devagiri rājas. Kanhar fort, near Patna probably takes its name from the same prince who flourished about 1150 A. D."[1]

10. KAILĀSA—Inscription 5 : Ceiling and architraves (North side) same date ?

"On the north side is a fight, from the left an army advances, in which is first, an elephant bearing a rājā, and behind him come men with drawn bows and arrows and others with sword and shield : the rājā's name, however, is lost. On the right, many men with sword and shield advance rapidly all with the sword arm stretched out, and pierced with arrows; all have beards and large eyes and may be intended to Muhammadans; over them is painted the word.

महमरलोकु (or मसमरलोकु)[2]

13 PĀRŚVANĀTHA ON THE HILL : Inscription (corrected) on the cushion of the image. A. D. 1234-1235.

[1] स्वस्ति श्री शाके ११५६ जयसंवत्सरे [फाल्गुण सुघत्रीति भाबुधे

श्रीवर्द्धनपुर ` ा. जभा ` ज्जनि राणुगिः ।
तत्पुत्रो म्हालुगिः स्वर्णाविल्लभो जगतोऽप्यभूत् ॥१॥
ताभ्यां बभूवुश्चत्वारः पुत्राश्चक्रेश्वरादयः ।
मुख्यश्चक्रेश्वरस्तेषु दानधर्मगुणोत्तरः ॥२॥

1. *Inscriptions of the Cave Temples* p.97.
2. *Ibid.*

ಗಂಗಪಗಳ ಮಗ
ವಗಯಣ್ಣನ ಬರಹ
ಶಕ ೧೩೧೨ ಶ್ರೀ

Kannada Inscription of Śaka 1312
(*in modern script*)

[*To face* p. 93

[2] चैत्यश्रीपार्श्वनाथस्य गिरौ चारणसेविते ।
चक्रेश्वरोऽसृजद्दानाद्घृताहुतीं च कर्मणाम् ।। ३ ।।
बहूनि बिम्बानि जिनेश्वराणां महान्ति तेनैव विरच्य सर्वतः ।
श्रीचारणाद्रिर्गमितः सुतीर्थतां कैलासभूभृद्भरतेन यद्वत् ।। ४ ।।
[3] धर्मैकमूर्तिः स्थिरशुद्धदृष्टिर्हृद्यो सतीवल्लभकल्पवृक्षः ।
उत्पद्यते निर्मलधर्मपालश्चक्रेश्वरः पञ्चमचक्रपाणिः ।। ५ ।।
शुभं भवतु ।। फाल्गुन त्रितीयां बुधे ।।

1. "Hail : in the year 1156 of the famous Śaka era, in the year (*of the Bṛihaspati cycle*) called Jaya. In Śrī Vardhanāpura was born Rāṇugi . . . . . . his son (*was*) Gālugi [Mhālugi] (*whose*) wife (*was*) Svarṇā (*dear*) also to the world.

2. From those two sprang four sons, Chakreśvara and the rest. Chakreśvara was chief among them excelling through the virtue of liberality.

3. He gave, on the hill that is frequented by Chāraṇas, a monument of Pārśvanātha, and by (*this act of*) liberality (*he made*) an oblation of his *karma* !

4. Many huge images of the lordly Jinas he made, and converted the Chāraṇādri thereby into a holy *tīrtha*, just as Bharata (*made*) Mount Kailāsa (*a tīrtha*).

5. The unique image of faith, of firm and pure convictions, kind, constant to his faithful wife, resembling the tree of paradise (*in liberality*) Chakreśvara becomes a protector of the pure faith, a fifth Vāsudeva. *Quod felix faustumque sit* ! Phalguna 3, Wednesday." [In the Chota Kailāsa an image dated A. D. 1247 was found, dedicated also by a Vardhanāpura man.][1]

13. KAILĀSA—Inscription 6, Saṁvat 1385, A. D. 1329, *padmāsana* of the entrance Gajalakṣmī.

संवत् १३८४ कार्तिकं वदि ...

"Probably the date here is also in the Śaka era, to which the characters agree".[2]

14 KAILĀSA—Inscription 7, *Śaka* 1312, A. D. 1390. On the base of the pilaster on the north or left side of the entrance to the hall (of the main temple) is a short inscription in three lines of Kannada, which reads :

1. *Inscriptions of the Cave Temples*. Translation pp. 99-100.
2. *Ibid.*, p. 98.

"The writing of Vagayaṇṇa, the son of Gaṅgapa. Śaka 1312. Śrī."[1]

15. KAILĀSA—Inscription 8. *Śaka* 1384, A. D. 1462. "Beside a *liṅga* on the right side of the porch are some four letters in the southern form of alphabet and of about same age [early in the 8th century]. On the other side is a painted inscription of Śaka 1384, below a *liṅga*, worshipped by Mārkaṇḍeya, and was probably written when the painting was renewed and the *liṅga* restored, after the last iconoclastic invasion of the Musalmāns."[2]

1. *Ibid.*, p. 97.
2. *Inscriptions of the Cave Temples*, *p*.98.

Illustration 7
CAVE 30 (J 2). Chota Kailas, view of temple tower.
C. A. D. 810-880.

[facing p. 95

Illustration 6
CAVE 30 (J 2). Chota Kailas, view showing unfinished forecourt.
C. A. D. 810-880.

[facing p. 95

APPENDIX II

THE KAILĀSA, UNITY OF CONCEPTION AND EXECUTION

It is necessary to know whether the Kailāsa was finished quickly or not,[1] to decide the date of the Jain caves; if it was, we have a clear *terminus a quo*, especially as other evidence points to the Jain caves being later than the Kailāsa. The great monolith temple has a remarkable regularity; to be convinced of this, all one has to do is to climb the hill and stand on the ridge at the back of the temple tower exactly behind its central finial, and from there draw an imaginary straight line towards the entrance gate. Also, it seems that these excavations were begun and finished in one operation. The Chhota Kailāsa, for instance, a much smaller structure, is unfinished, and so are much smaller caves : it appears that when funds ran out the work was stopped for good (see Illustrations 6 and 7). If this is true of small temples, it is even more so of a big one; hence, if the finances were not adequate from the very beginning for an enormous undertaking like the Kailāsa, it is doubtful if anybody would have bothered to go on from where the previous patron had left off.

(i) *Size*

The enormous size of the Kailāsa "excludes the possibility of its having been excavated and sculptured within fifteen years of Krishnarāja's reign."[2] Such is the opinion of Goetz.

(ii) *Technical resources*

Those "then available had to keep in bounds even the ambitions of such a strong ruler."[3]

1. H. Goetz, "The Kailāsa of Ellora and the Chronology of Rāshṭrakūṭa Art", *Artibus Asiae* XV (1952), pp. 84-107.
2. *Ibid.*, p. 86.
3. *Ibid.*

(iii) *Variety af styles*

Goetz claims that there are at least ten in the Kailāsa.[1] Different styles *simultaneously* in operation, he contends, fuse and become indistinguishable; when they are applied *successively*, they maintain their identity.[2] But the styles at the Kailāsa are distinguishable, hence they must have occurred in a time sequence.

Having made these points, Goetz[3] goes on to outline the method whereby the probable date of each style can be detected, which needs the following to be noted :

(iv) *The technical process of excavating the caves.* This starts from above to the ground at the bottom, and from the sides of the hill towards its inside. Hence a part that is on a higher level must be earlier in date than that which is below it.[4]

(v) *Stylistic confrontations*

Given (a) the similarities of a work of art in one region to other works in a style functioning in another region, and (b) the contact between the peoples of these regions, that work of art can have been executed only after the contact.[5] The important styles and confrontations are the following.[6]

a. The original Ellora style of the Dashāvatāra, of the passage of the entrance to the Kailāsa, and of that between the main temple and the Nandi pavilion. This has no clear confrontation.[7]

b. The Cālukya and Pallava styles of the Kailāsa temple tower, and some of the temple's other parts. Contact

1. *Ibid.*
2. *Ibid.*, footnote 5.
3. *Ibid.*, footnote 9.
4. *Ibid.*, *p.* 89.
5. *Ibid.*, "And likewise in other states, the influence of these campaigns can be traced in art".
6. Summary on *ibid.*, p. 107.
7. *Ibid.*, p. 92.

with these styles was real only after the annexation of places like Pattadakal and Kanchi.[1]

c. The Eastern Cālukya style of the chapel of the River Goddesses. Contact established by Dhruva.[2]

d. The Pratihāra style of the chapel of the Mother Goddesses, whose influx cannot be anterior to Govinda III's campaigns against that dynasty.[3]

e. Lankeshvara : Rāṣṭrakūṭa Baroque. No confrontation.[4]

f. The Cāhamāna, Kachhwaha, Chandella and Kalacuri styles discernible in the large relief of the Kailāsatolana (near the Mother Goddesses) and parts of the lower storey of the Nandi pavilion. It was Kṛṣṇa III who came in contact with the habitats of these styles.[5] The "later work" of the Jain Indra Sabha cave also smacks of this style.[6]

g. The Paramāra and late Pratihāra styles, in the frieze of lions and elephants. Its sculptors must have in some way known of the Nīlakaṇṭheśvara temple of Udaypur, whose region was annexed by the megalomaniac Kṛṣṇa III.[7]

(*vi*) *Extraordinariness of conception*

Proportions in one work of art, which are strange when compared with those of other known works, are probably more afterthoughts than integral to the original idea. The lions and elephants plinth has no known precedent, and hence surely cannot have been envisaged by the original architect.

(*vii*) *Structural peculiarities*

When several parts of a complex do not cohere, it points to the probable absence of a homogeneous plan. Now the structural peculiarities of some of the parts of the Kailāsa complex indicate that they were either accessible from levels now removed, and in some cases the means of access show later and clumsy adjustments. "All the halls. . .in the cliffs. . .

1. *Ibid.*, pp. 93-94.
2. *Ibid.*, p. 99. No Eastern Cālukya monument is referred to.
3. *Ibid.*, pp. 99-100.
4. *Ibid.*, pp. 102. There is no confrontation with Lankeshvara.
5. *Ibid.*, pp. 104-105.
6. *Ibid.*, p. 107.
7. *Ibid.*, pp. 105-107.

open outside as if they have originally been accessible from there. The later masons have never dared completely to remove the stone ledges outside those former entrances; but there is no evidence for the former existence of stone bridges between these halls and the great vimāna. Moreover, the staircases which at present lead up from the court to those halls, are so clumsily set in, that it is quite evident that they represent later adjustments."[1]

Critique

The first two basic assumptions, about *size* and *technical resources*, are too weak to sustain so much theorizing. India was then one of the richest countries of the civilized world, yet unpillaged by the Turkish marauders. Of the three prominent imperial dynasties of the time in India, the Rāṣṭrakūṭas were the most powerful, and had an empire whose hard core comprised Central India and the deep south. We do not know how much it cost to excavate rock temples in those days, but one imagines that a ruler of such extensive territory would not find the expenditure an intolerable burden. True, the scale was unusual for a rock temple, and (according to Karka's grant) it caused surprise to the architect himself, but only after he had seen the structure completed.

The fact behind the third assumption, the *variety of styles*, is true. Stylistic differences are distinguishable, though they are perhaps not so many as to constitute ten clear groups. The assumption based on this fact is, however, fallacious. The styles of the painters on the walls of the Sistine chapel (even before Michelangelo took charge of the ceiling) did not fuse because they happened to be working together and the details in Maderna's additions to St. Peter's are not different from Michelangelo's just because Maderna happened to work on the building after Buonarotti's death.

The fourth assumption on the *technical processes*, is both indisputable, and suicidal for Goetz's theories. The earlier sculptures can only be on the upper and outer levels; but the entrance passage to the Kailāsa and the passage between the Nandi pavilion and the main temple are on the building's lowest

1. *Ibid.*, p. 96.

level, and (according to Goetz himself)[1] are among its earliest excavations. The presence of the Gajalakṣmī inscription testifies to this. Hence, the lowest level of the present building was envisaged from the very start, and what is more soon reached by excavation. From this it follows that the architect had in mind (a) the two passages mentioned; and hence passages inseparable from its lower storey, and the top storey could not have been added later; *ergo* (c) he also planned the bridges above the two passages, connecting the upper storey of the Nandi maṇḍapa, the first floor of the entrance gateway, and the body of the main temple; (d) further, too, the temple tower (for obvious reasons) and the subsidiary chapels which are on the same level as the upper storey of the Nandi pavilion, were items in the original plan. Lastly (e) the elephants and the two free-standing pillars are integral to this plan. Not only are their proportions just right for them not to have been planned as smaller monuments, and not only are they and the elephants inconceivable as later additions, but they belong to the lowest level, and hence had evidently been planned from the beginning. In fact, any one who accepts Goetz's hypothesis is obliged to admit that, except perhaps for the plinth, the whole of the Kailāsa was planned from the start, and swiftly executed.

The fifth assumption, *stylistic confrontation* is, in the abstract, of great service to art; but it must be shown that there was no real contact previous to the postulated date. More concretely, it must be proved that the Rāṣṭrakūṭas did not conquer the habitats of the several Northern and Southern styles long before the dates which Goetz assigns to the parts of Ellora which the contacts supposedly inspired. Yet it is obvious that contact was established with the regions of the principal styles from almost the very start, and certainly by Kṛṣṇa I's time. Unless shown to be otherwise, the possibility of sculptors having come from the various regions under Kṛṣṇa has to be taken for granted; postulating also that, apart from Pattadakal and Kanchi, the confrontations can be labelled with the certainty that Goetz appears to possess.

1. *Ibid.*, pp. 89-90.

The sixth assumption, *extraordinariness of conception*, is also both groundless and self-destructive. The architect of Ellora was as audacious an artist as any in the history of world art. Yet his audacity was not as much as Goetz claims for him; for it would have been odd indeed had he conceived a double-storeyed maṇḍapa joined to a temple perched on a higher level. At it is, he only chose to have a larger plinth with caryatids more colossal than usual. It is orthodox to have a plinth; size only creates a difference in degree. But a building with different levels cut according to Goetz's specification would both be a structure wholly without precedent and give us a building totally devoid of the present one's coherence and monumentality.

The last assumption based on *structural peculiarities* does not also bear examination. One must keep in mind (a) that the primary intention of the architect, in excavating the part of the hill where the Kailāsa stands, was to excavate the Kailāsa, and not the adjacent cave temples, and (b) that if ideas conforming to the primary plan conflict with those consistent with the secondary plans, the latter must be made to harmonize with the former, and not the other way around. None of the levels which go well with the halls in the cliffs are consistent with the present shape of the temple : either the temple tower would have to be half-submerged in the rock, or the hall of the main temple left unfinished at an embarrassingly low level for the columns. In other words, the levels consistent with the cliff halls would touch the main temple at the strangest points. It is enough to imagine that they may have been intended to be excavations of little consequence, and thus allowed to become inaccessible or intended to be reached by a ledge with steps sideways. Plans of this kind could later have been abandoned. Apart from the lack of evidence of bridges (from the temple tower to these halls), the very thought of having them would be unutterably foolish, not only because of the disfigurement they would bring on the tower, but also because that structure is a solid body, and the users of the bridge would have to scale the one to get to the other—an operation which would require considerable athletic expertise. On the whole this theory, wild as it otherwise is, can be taken as a good example of imprecise speculation posing as empirical reasoning.

The Kailāsa's importance justifies a painstaking analysis of the problem of its unity, for it is the culmination of the grand style of the Dashāvatāra, the Do Thal and Tin Thal. The echoes of the *terribilita* of Elephanta find their source here; its power dessicates the sap of fresh ideas and of the naturalness that so pulsates in the Rameshvara series, and the urge for a rigid pattern-book elegance becomes more insistent. We can in it already visualize the shape that the Jain caves will take.

APPENDIX III

THE KONKANI ORIGIN OF THE RĀṢṬRAKŪṬAS

Of the dynasties that patronized the Jains, none were more illustrious and powerful than the Rāṣṭrakūṭas; so their origin cannot be lacking in interest. Since I completed the book in 1969, I have come across facts that leave me in no doubt that they were Konkani *kṣatriyas*. These styled themselves "four-chariot warriors" (*catūrathi*, Konkani *chāraḍo*, plural *chāraḍe*, Punjabi *chaḍḍā*), or "fighters" (*rāṇaka*, Konkani *rāṇo*, plural *rāṇe*). This thesis, ably demonstrated by Varde Valaulikar (1877-1946), has generally escaped the notice of scholars. The following is mostly a summary of his arguments.[1]

Our main clue is the title that the Rāṣṭrakūṭas constantly gave themselves, "Lords of the noble Laṭṭalūra (or Lattalūra) town", *Laṭṭalūrapuravarādhīśa*[2]. There seems to be no other such town except Loṭalī or Loṭḷī in Sāṣṭī, Goa, renowned for its wealth and intellect. The transformation of *Laṭṭalūrapura* into *Loṭli* is inevitable, if we subject the former word to the phonetic laws of Prakrit and Konkani. But we must first bear in mind that *Laṭṭalūrapura* is a tautology, as *ūra* (in Dravidian languages) and *pura* (in Sanskrit) both mean "town". It is thus enough to say either *Laṭṭala pura* or *Laṭṭala ūra*. The latter may then be phonetically combined to form *Laṭṭalūra* or *Laṭṭalaura*. Then *Laṭṭala* can become *Loṭṭala*, since *a* can be transformed into *o* according to Vararuci's *Prākṛtaprakāśa* 1 : 6,7. It can then be simplified into *Loṭala*. *Loṭala*, in turn, can become *Loṭalī*, for, in Konkani, place names can have masculine or feminine terminations, preferably the latter. The modern capital of Goa is called *Paṇaja* (pronounced *Paṇaz*), but more

1. V.R. Varde Valaulikar, *Goykarāṃlī Goyāṁbāili Vasṇūk*, Bombay : Gomantak Printing Press, 1928, pp. 28-39 and 71-72; and *Kāhiṁ Marāṭhī Lekh*, Bombay, same press, 1945, pp. 275-280.

2. Sirur and Nilgund Inscriptions of Amoghavarṣa, *Indian Antiquary* 12, p. 218, and *Epigraphia Indica* 6, p. 102.

often *Paṇaji*. Most modern Indian tongues drop the middle *a*, and *Paṇaji* is usually pronounced *Paṇji*, and *Loṭali Loṭli*.

It is generally claimed that *Laṭṭalūra* is the modern *Lāṭūr*, in the Deccan, and that the change of the former word into the latter is as follows :

Lattalura, *Latalura*, *Latal ura*, *Latlur*, *Lattur*, *Lāṭūr*.[1] This is fanciful. *Latlur* can only become *Lallur*, never *Latlur*, according to Pāṇini 8 : 4 : 60, as *bhagavat*+*līlā* can only become *bhagavallīlā*, and never *bhagavatlīlā*. As to how Lāṭūr's renown compares with that of Loṭḷi, I am unable to say.

However, let us grant that Laṭṭalūra can phonetically transform into either Lāṭur or Loṭli. Have we other facts, social, religious, or the like, to help us decide the issue ? Luckily, we do, and they are provided by the Sitabadi inscription.[2] There we are told that the Cālukya Tribhuvanamalla, or Vikramāditya VI (whose daughter, Mailala, as we know from other sources, was married to the Goa Kadamba Jayakeśi), had two officials, both "emigrants from Lattalaura", *Lattalauravinirgata*. One was "the Mahāsāmanta Dhāḍibaḍaka Rāṇaka, emigrant from Lattalaura, sprung from the great Rāṣṭrakūṭa family . . . blessed with peace through Cāmuṇḍā's favour". The other was "the Daṇḍanāyaka Śrī Vāsudeva, emigrant from Lattalaura, member of the Kāṇva *śākhā* and the Vatsa *gotra* . . . his great-grandfather was Vīṭha Pai, his grandfather Bopa Pai, and he (himself) was Bhaṭṭa Padmanābha's son . . . he was blessed with peace through Narasiṁha's grace". All this reveals the following facts :

(1) That the Rāṣṭrakūṭa Dhāḍibhaḍaka and his colleague Vāsudeva Pai were both emigrants from Lattalaura;

(2) that the latter had a family name found only among Koṅkaṇī Sārasvat Brahmins—*Pai* (Skt *pati*, Maharastri *paī*) ;

(3) that this person, Vāsudeva Pai, belonged to a *śākhā* and a *gotra* common among Koṅkaṇī Sārasvats;[3]

(4) that the Rāṣṭrakūṭa Dhāḍibhaḍaka was a *rāṇaka*, and thus apparently a Konkani *rāṇo*;

1. Fleet, in *Epigraphia Indica* 7, p. 226.
2. *Epigraphia Indica* 3, p. 306
3. See S.S. Talmaki, *Saraswat Families*, Bombay, part 2 (1939) and part 3 (1951).

(5) that both formed the typically and traditionally Konkani Sārasvat-Chārado partnership;

(6) that Vāsudeva's family deity was Narasiṁha (*Nārasiṅgha*), and Dhāḍibhaḍaka's Cāmuṇḍā. These deities, worshipped by Chāraḍe and Sārasvats, had temples in Loṭḷi's environs, as at Veling and Sāṅkvāl (Śaṅkhāvalī);[1]

(7) that their king, intimately related as he was to the Konkani ruling house (of the Kadambas)—through his daughter's marriage—could well be expected to have Konkani officials.

It seems to follow, then, that the Lattalaura of our two emigrants is inevitably a Konkani town, and hence none other than the renowned Loṭḷi.

All these facts intimately link Laṭṭala with the Konkan, and are confirmed by still another fact—that Kṛṣṇa I's son, Govinda II, was born on a hill named *Indubimba*,[2] "the disk of the moon" (*indu = candra*). It is still a custom for Konkani husbands, living outside the Konkan, to send their wives to their native villages for childbirth. There seems to be no other Disk-of-the-Moon Hill besides *Candrabimba*, the site of a Kadamba victory,[3] which is the same as Chandravāḍī in Zāṁbāulī in Goa. It has a hill known as the "Mountain" (*parvata*, Konkani *porvot*), celebrated in Konkani folklore,[4] and crowned by a temple to the Moon god, Candranātha. True to his Konkani origins and sentiment, the great patron of the Kailāsa, "lord of the noble town of Loṭḷi", sent his wife to the noblest temple in Loṭḷi's vicinity, that of the Moon god who adorns the crest of Śiva, lord of Kailāsa.

1. *Konkaṇākhyāna*, quoted by Valaulikar, *Kāhīṁ Marāṭhī Lekh*, p. 280.
2. *Indian Antiquary* 12, p. 247
3. *Epigraphia Indica* 3, p. 299. *Indian Antiquary* 9, pp. 24-35.
4. See Jose Pereira and Michael Martins, *A Sheaf of Deknnis*, Bombay: The Konkan Cultural Association, 1967, pp. 11 and 18.

PLANS—A

THE TEMPLES

NOTE ON THE PLANS

The plans are schematical versions of the older and accurate plans of the Archaeological Survey of India—except for nos. 2, 6-11, 18, 20 and 31, which are sketch plans. In the placement of the themes I have sought to avoid abbreviation, except in the three following instances, which represent the most frequently recurring themes of the Ellora Jain temples :

T Tīrthaṅkara

S Seated sage (tīrthaṅkara, arhat or siddha)

EE Erect or standing sage

The titles of the themes, for reasons of space, are briefer in the plans than they are in the inventories facing them, as for instance, "Pārśva's Temptation" instead of "Pārśvanātha's Temptation."

Ellora Jain Temples Plan

एलापुरचारणाद्रिजिनालयचक्रम

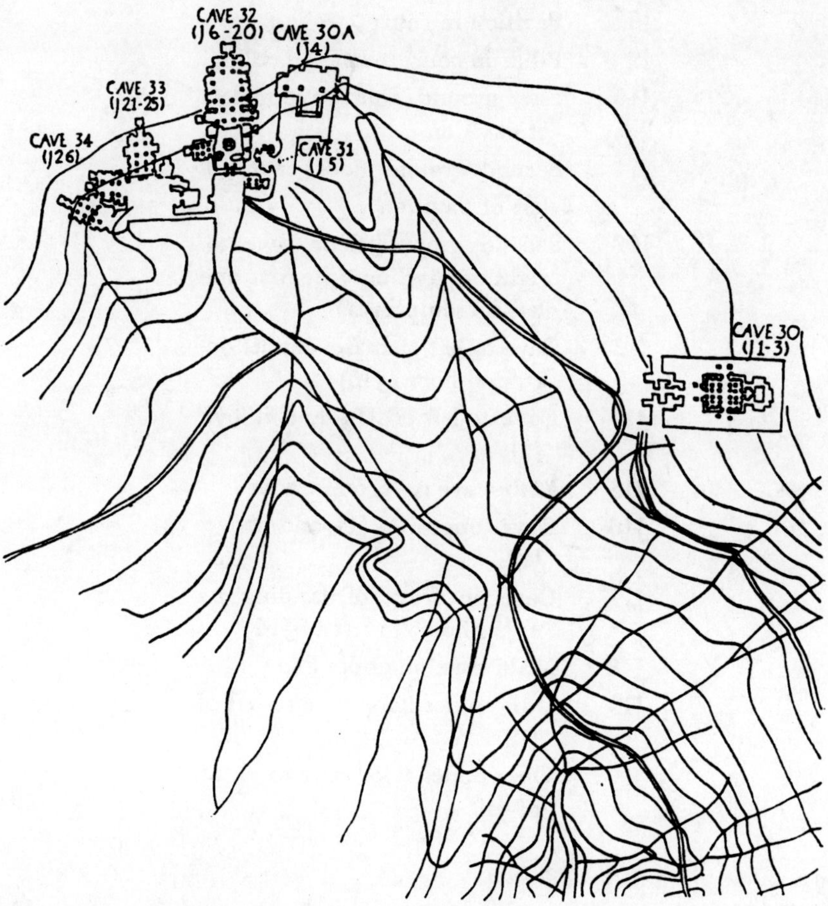

Burgess' numbering	*Revised numbering*	*Identificatian*	*Name of temple*
1	2	3	4
30	J1	Entrance screen of Chota Kailāsa	Chota Kailāsa
	J2	The temple	
	J3	Cave to the right of temple	
30a	J4	Cave with projecting porch	
	J5	Cave below 30a	
31	J6	Cave 31	
32	J7	Entrance gate	Indra Sabha
	J8	Pavilion in court	
	J9	Pillar in court to left of pavilion	
	J10	First ground floor cave to left of pavilion	
	J11	Second ground floor cave to left of pavilion	
	J12	Second ground floor cave to right of pavilion (the first one has no sculptures)	
	J13	Cave to left of main chapel on ground floor (J15)	
	J14	Cave to left of J14 and above J11	
	J15	Main cave on ground floor	
	J16	Cave opposite J14 and above J12	
	J17	Cave in front of landing to upper floor, to left of J14	
	J18	Main cave on upper floor	
	J19	Only upper floor cave to left of J18	
	J20	Only upper floor cave to right of J18	

1	2	3	4
33	J21	Upper floor main cave	Jagannātha Sabhā
	J22	Cave to the left of the stairway on descending ; to the right of the entrance to main ground floor cave (J24)	
	J23	Subsidiary ground floor cave, front right of main ground floor cave (J24)	
	J24	Main ground floor cave, front left of ground floor caves	
	J25	Cave to left of entrance to J24	
34	J26	Cave to left of J25	
35	J27	Pārśvanātha monolithic statue	
35	J28	Doorway near steps leading from J27 to J29	
	J29	Small square monolith temple	
	J30	Small temple below J29, flanked by an elephant with warriors on each side	
	J31	Stairway of J30	
	J32	Small rectangular temple to front right of J30	

Points to be noted

1. The names Indra Sabhā and Jagannātha Sabhā are applied primarily to J18 and J21 respectively, and only secondarily to the complex of caves linked with them.

2. It is possible to visit J32-J34, once one has entered J32 through J31, without retracing one's steps. This is because a door leads from J29 (one of the Indra Sabhā caves) to J21 (Jagannātha Sabhā), and from J33 (one of the Jagannātha Sabhā group) to J26.

Cave 30A

Fig 1-3

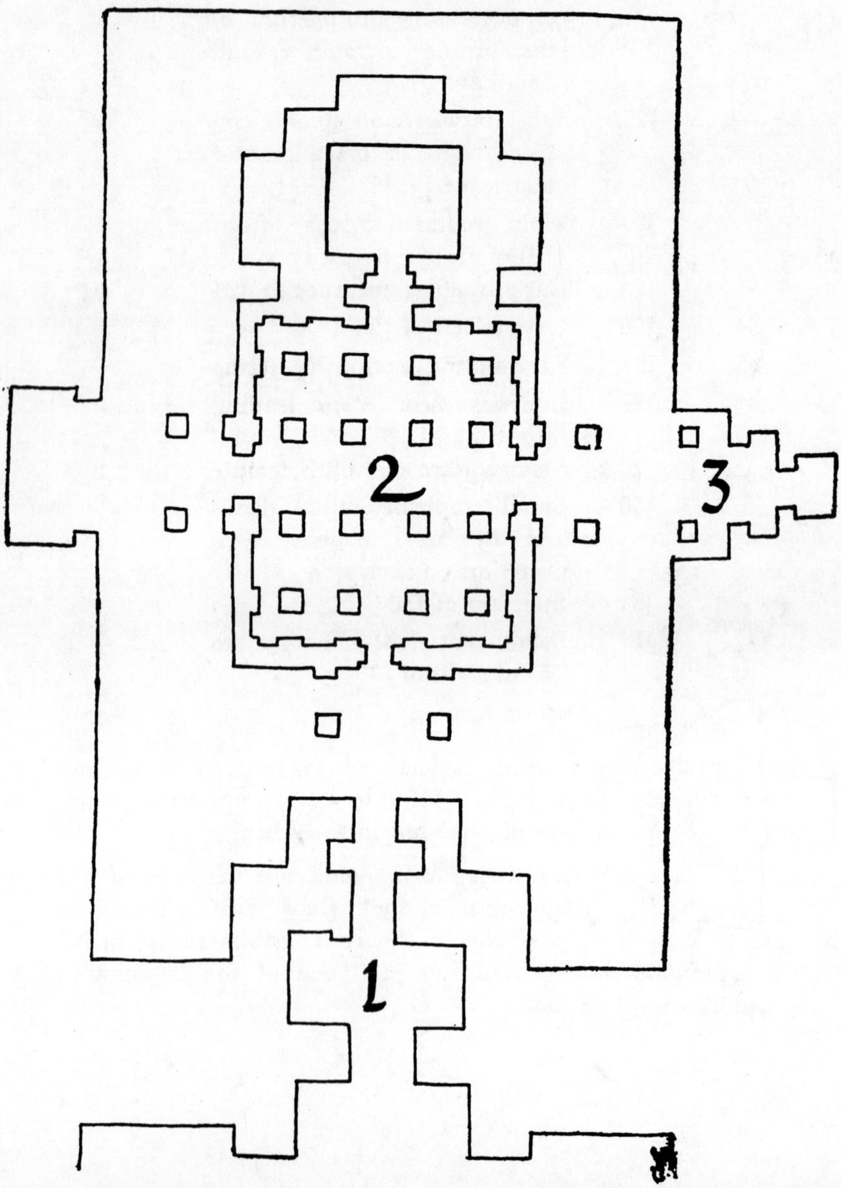

Cave 32, First storey (J6 - 17)

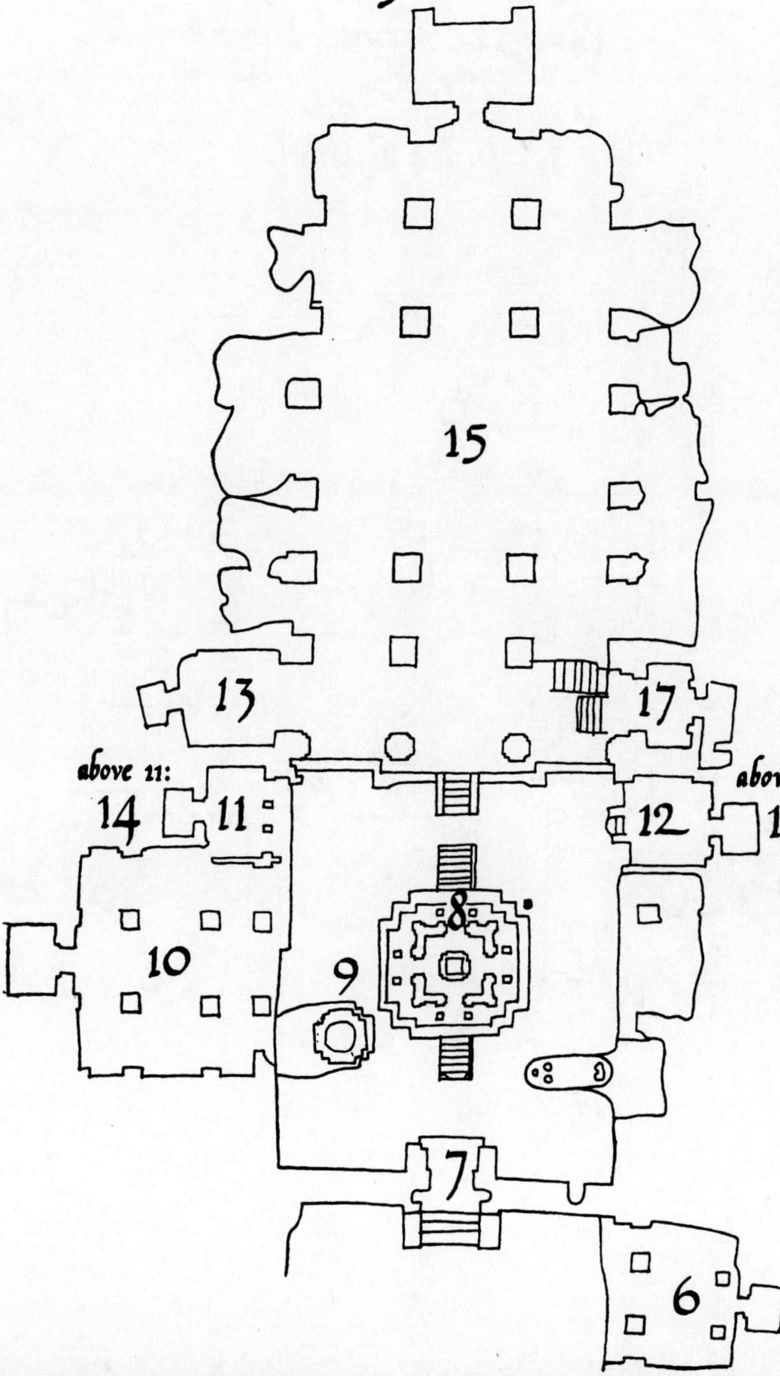

Cave 32, second storey
(J 18-20)
"Indra Sabhā"

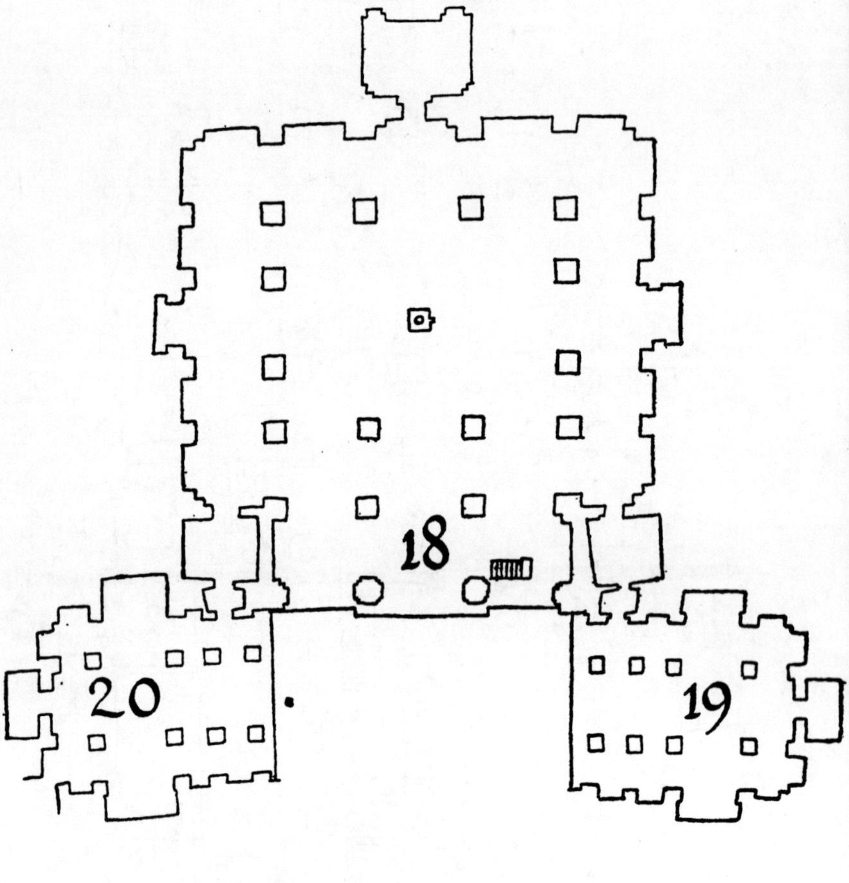

Cave 33. second Storey (J 21) "Jagannātha Sabhā"

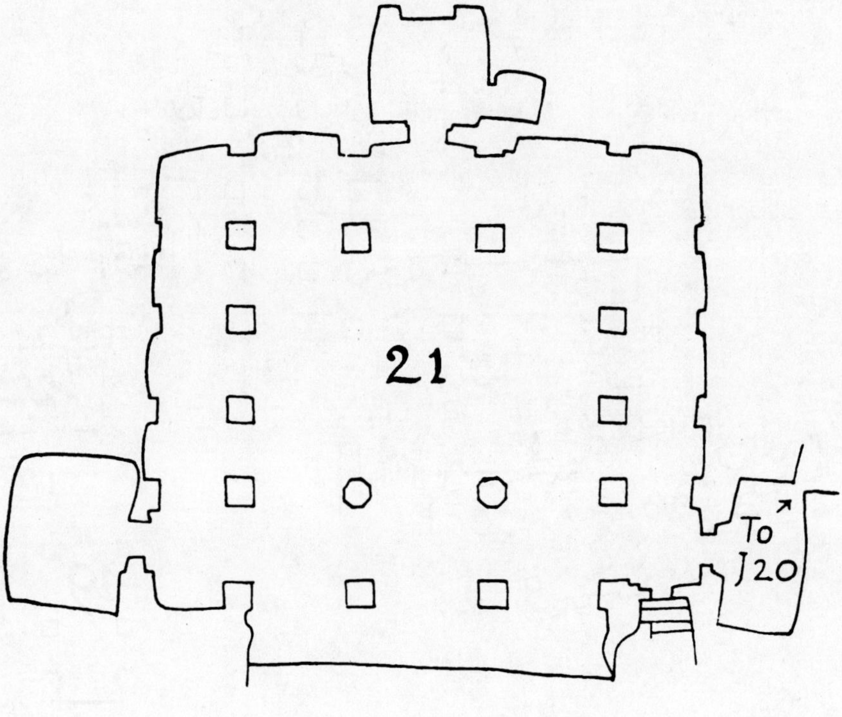

Cave 33 first storey (J22-25)
& Cave 34 (J26)

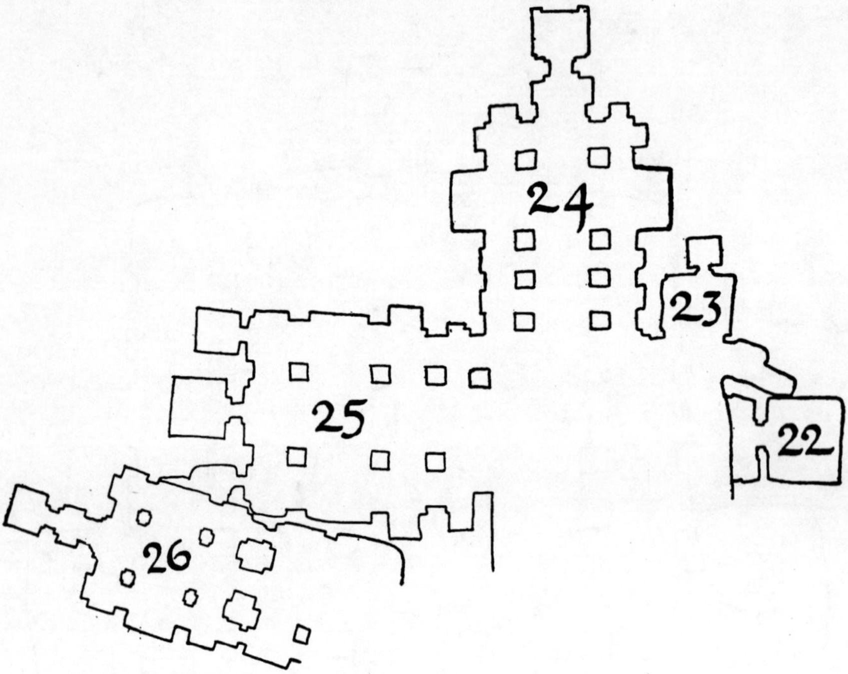

Yādava Caves (27–32)

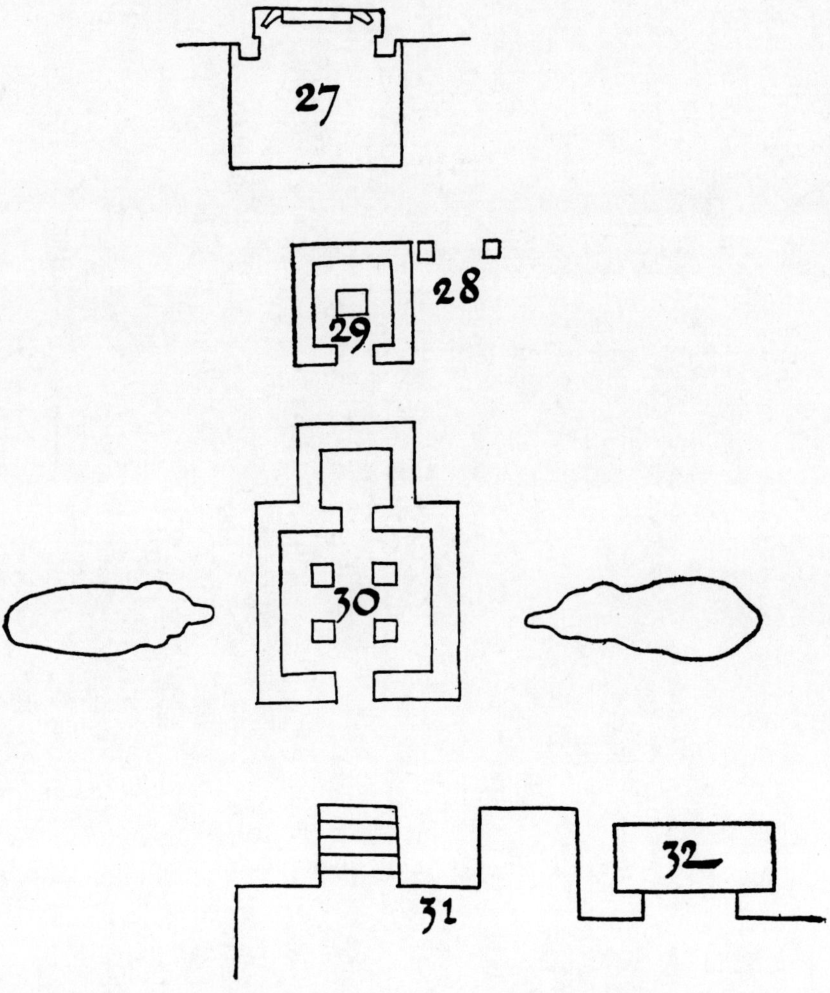

PLANS—B

THE THEMES IN THE TEMPLES

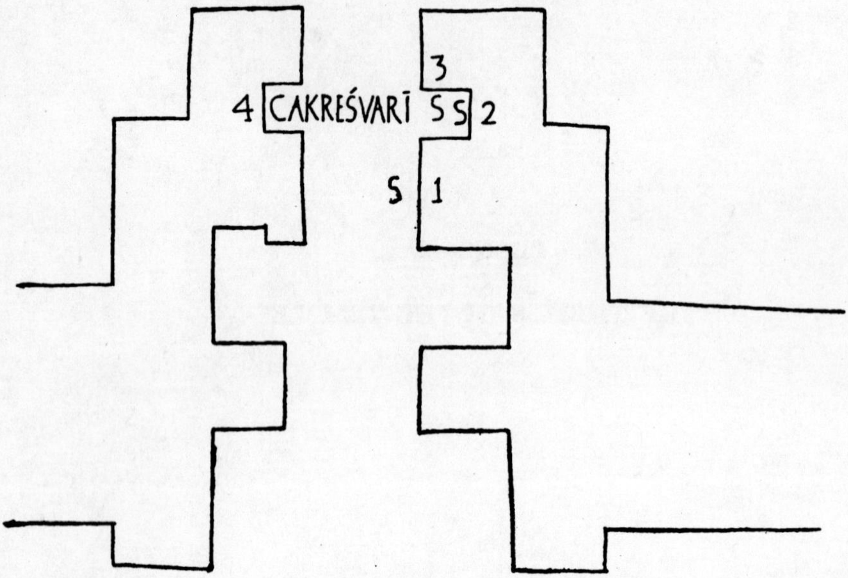
3
4
CAKREŚVARĪ
S
S
2
S
1

J 1

1 Seated tīrthaṅkara
2 Seated tīrthaṅkara
3 Seated tīrthaṅkara
4 Cakreśvarī

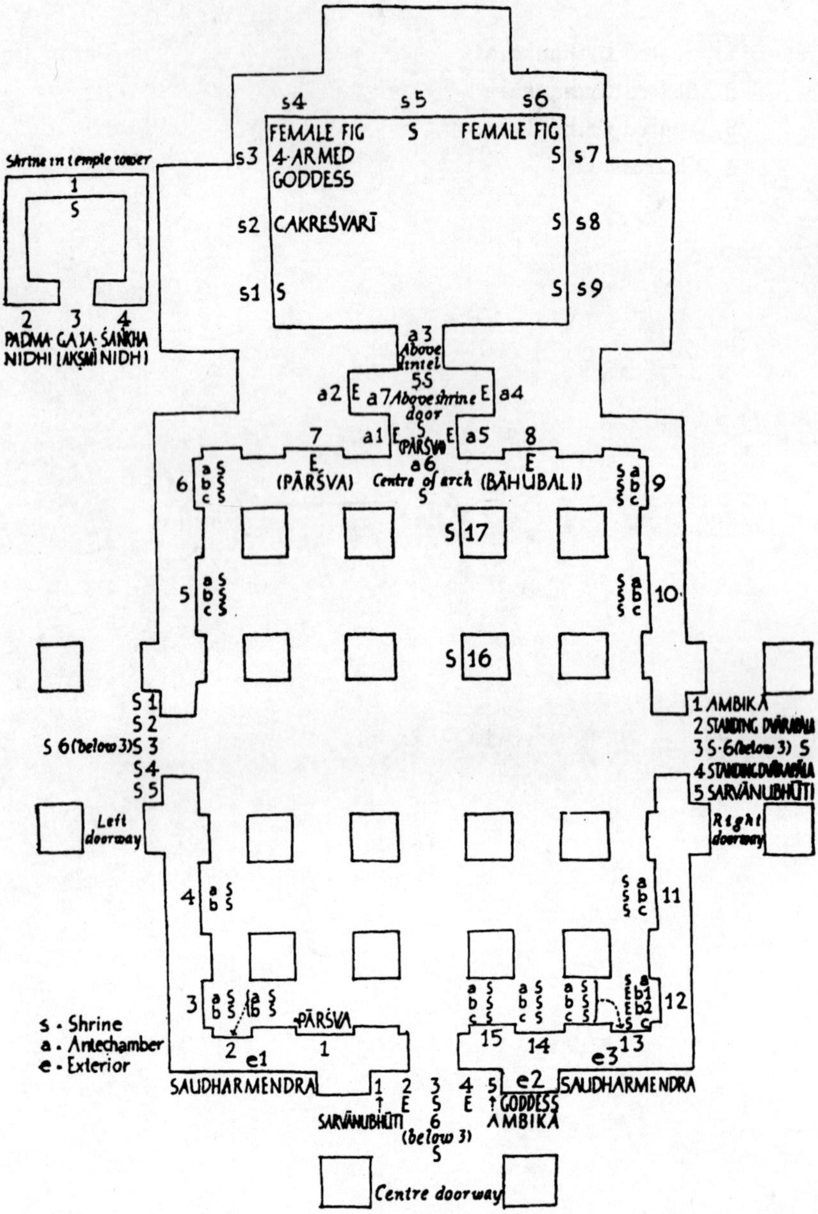
Shrine in temple tower
1 S
2 3 4
PADMA-NIDHI GAJA-LAKṢMĪ ŚAṄKHA-NIDHI
s4 s5 s6
FEMALE FIG S FEMALE FIG
s3 4-ARMED GODDESS
S s7
s2 CAKREŚVARĪ
S s8
s1 S
S s9
a3 Above lintel
S S
a2 E a7 Above shrine door E a4
7 a1 E S (PĀRŚVA) E a5 8
E a6 E
(PĀRŚVA) Centre of arch (BĀHUBALI)
S
6 a b c S S S
S S S a b c 9
S 17
5 a b c S S S
S S S a b c 10
S 16
S 1 S 2 S 6 (below 3) S 3 S 4 S 5
1 AMBIKĀ
2 STANDING DVĀRAPĀLA
3 S-6 (below 3) S
4 STANDING DVĀRAPĀLA
5 SARVĀNUBHŪTI
Left doorway
Right doorway
4 a b S S
S S S a b c 11
3 a b S S a b S S
PĀRŚVA
a b c S S S
a b c S S S
a b c S S S
S E E S a b1 b2 c 12
2 e1 1
15 14 13 e3
SAUDHARMENDRA
1 2 3 4 5 e2
SAUDHARMENDRA
E S E
SARVĀNUBHŪTI 6 (below 3) S
GODDESS AMBIKĀ
Centre doorway
S - Shrine
a - Antechamber
e - Exterior

J 2

EXTERIOR

FACADE

E 1 Saudharmendra
E 2 Goddess
E 3 Saudharmendra

DOORWAYS

Centre doorway

Figures above lintel

1 Sarvānubhūti
2 Standing tīrthaṅkara
3 Seated tīrthaṅkara
4 Standing tīrthaṅkara
5 Ambikā
6 (*below* 3, *on doorpost*) Seated tīrthaṅkara

Left doorway

Figures above lintel

1 Seated tīrthaṅkara
2 Standing tīrthaṅkara
3 Seated tīrthaṅkara
4 Standing tīrthaṅkara
5 Seated tīrthaṅkara
6 (*below* 3, *on doorpost*) Seated tīrthaṅkara

Right doorway

Figures above lintel

1 Sarvānubhūti
2 Standing tīrthaṅkara
3 Seated tīrthaṅkara
4 Standing tīrthaṅkara
5 Ambikā
6 (*below* 3, *on doorpost*) Seated tīrthaṅkara

INTERIOR

TEMPLE HALL

1	Pārśvanātha
2a	Seated tīrthaṅkara
b	Seated tīrthaṅkara
3a	Seated tīrthaṅkara
b	Seated tīrthaṅkara
4a	Seated tīrthaṅkara
b	Seated tīrthaṅkara
5a	Seated tīrthaṅkara
b	Seated tīrthaṅkara
c	Seated tīrthaṅkara
6a	Seated tīrthaṅkara
b	Seated tīrthaṅkara
c	Seated tīrthaṅkara
7	Pārśvanātha standing
8	Bāhubali standing
9a	Seated tīrthaṅkara
b	Seated tīrthaṅkara
c	Seated tīrthaṅkara
10a	Seated tīrthaṅkara
b	Seated tīrthaṅkara
c	Seated tīrthaṅkara
11a	Seated tīrthaṅkara
b	Seated tīrthaṅkara
c	Seated tīrthaṅkara
12a	Seated tīrthaṅkara
b1	Standing tīrthaṅkara
b2	Standing tīrthaṅkara
c	Seated tīrthaṅkara
13a	Seated tīrthaṅkara
b	Seated tīrthaṅkara
c	Seated tīrthaṅkara
14a	Seated tīrthaṅkara
b	Seated tīrthaṅkara
c	Seated tīrthaṅkara
15	Seated tīrthaṅkara
16	Seated tīrthaṅkara
17	Seated tīrthaṅkara

ANTECHAMBER TO SHRINE

A 1 Standing tīrthaṅkara
A 2 Standing tīrthaṅkara
A 3 above lintel : Five seated tīrthaṅkaras (each in a compartment)
A 4 Standing tīrthaṅkara
A 5 Standing tīrthaṅkara
A 6 Arch in front of shrine : Seated tīrthaṅkara
A 7 above shrine door : Seated Pārśvanātha

SHRINE

S 1 Seated tīrthaṅkara
S 2 Cakreśvarī
S 3 4-armed goddess
S 4 Female figure
S 5 Seated tīrthaṅkara
S 6 Female figure
S 7 Seated tīrthaṅkara
S 8 Seated tīrthaṅkara
S 9 Seated tīrthaṅkara

SHRINE IN TEMPLE TOWER

1 Seated tīrthaṅkara
2 Padmanidhi
3 Gajalakṣmī
4 Śaṅkhanidhi

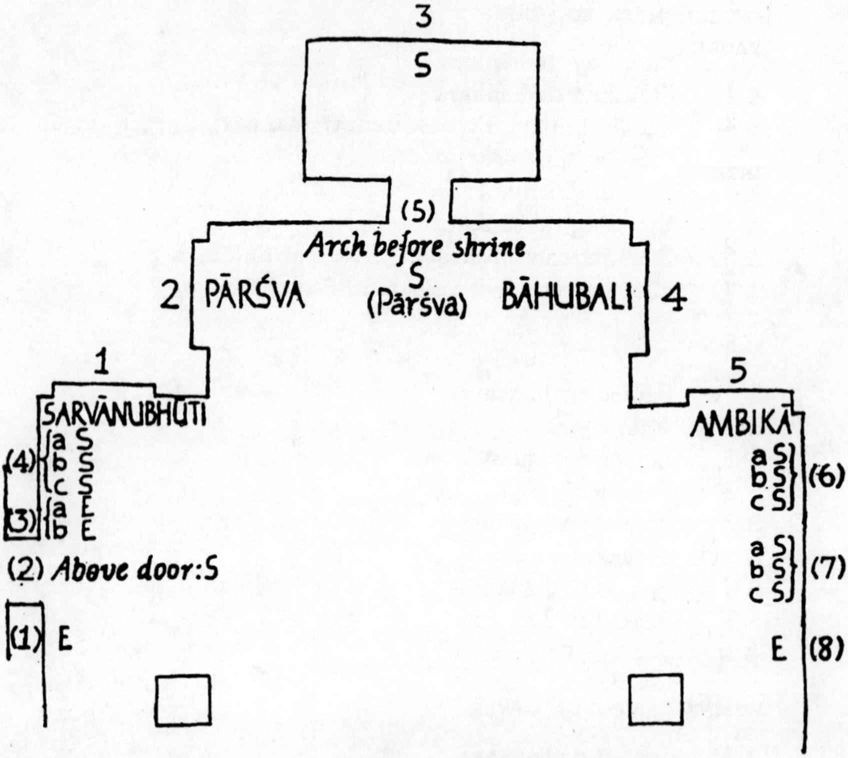
3
S
(5)
Arch before shrine
2 PĀRŚVA
S
(Pārśva)
BĀHUBALI 4
1
SARVĀNUBHŪTI
(4) a S
b S
c S
(3) a E
b E
(2) Above door: S
(1) E
5
AMBIKĀ
a S
b S
c S (6)
a S
b S
c S (7)
E (8)

Façade

1
S
2
SEATED YAKṢA: SARVĀNUBHŪTI?

J 3

FACADE

1 Seated tīrthaṅkara
2 Seated *yakṣa* (Sarvānubhūti ?)

INTERIOR

1 Sarvānubhūti
2 Pārśvanātha
3 Seated tīrthaṅkara
4 Bāhubali
5 Ambikā

(1) Standing tīrthaṅkara

(2) Above door : Seated tīrthaṅkara

(3) a Standing tīrthaṅkara
b Standing tīrthaṅkara

(4) a Seated tīrthaṅkara
b Seated tīrthaṅkara
c Seated tīrthaṅkara

(5) Arch before shrine : Pārśvanātha seated

(6) a Seated tīrthaṅkara
b Seated tīrthaṅkara
c Seated tīrthaṅkara

(7) a Seated tīrthaṅkara
b Seated tīrthaṅkara
c Seated tīrthaṅkara

(8) Standing tīrthaṅkara

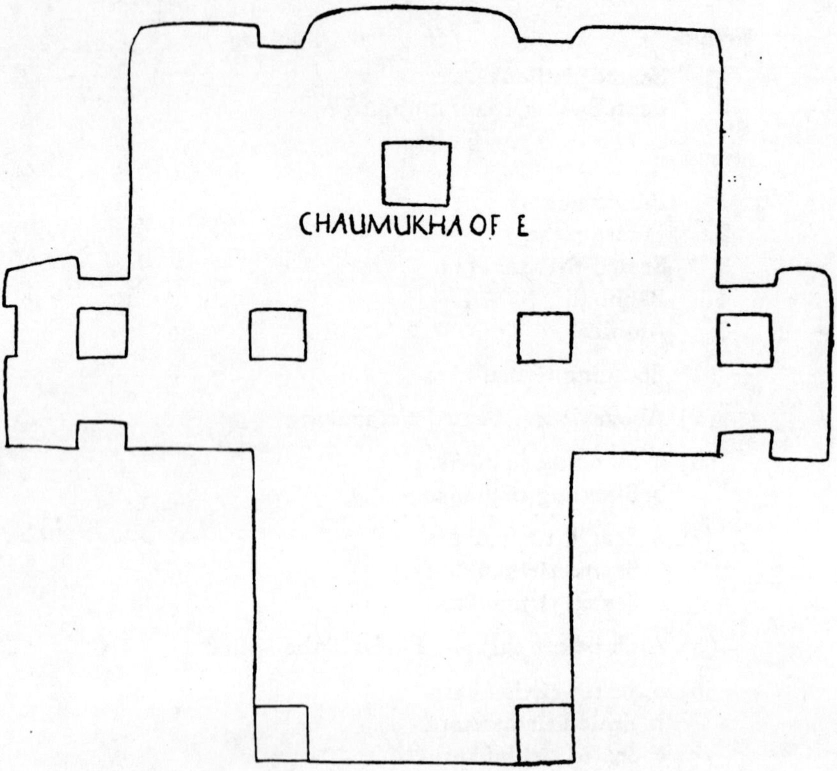
CHAUMUKHA OF E

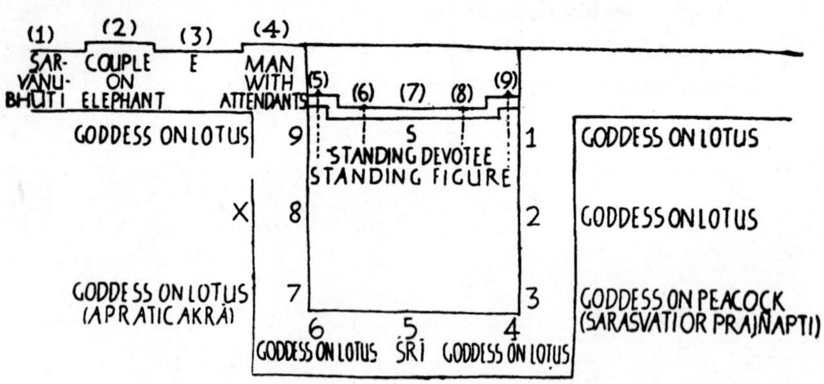
(1)
SAR-
VĀNU-
BHŪTI
(2)
COUPLE
ON
ELEPHANT
(3)
E
(4)
MAN
WITH
ATTENDANTS
(5)
(6)
(7)
(8)
(9)
S
STANDING DEVOTEE
STANDING FIGURE
GODDESS ON LOTUS
9
1
GODDESS ON LOTUS
X
8
2
GODDESS ON LOTUS
GODDESS ON LOTUS
(APRATICAKRĀ)
7
3
GODDESS ON PEACOCK
(SARASVATI OR PRAJÑAPTI)
6
5
4
GODDESS ON LOTUS
ŚRĪ
GODDESS ON LOTUS

J 4

INTERIOR

Chaumukha of 4 standing tīrthaṅkaras

ROOF OF PORCH

1 Goddess on lotus
2 Goddess on lotus
3 Sarasvatī or Prajñapti
4 Goddess on lotus
5 Śrī or Gajalakṣmī
6 Goddess on lotus
7 Goddess on lotus (Apraticakrā)
8 X ?
9 Goddess on lotus

PORCH ATTIC

(1) Figure on elephant : Sarvānubhūti ?
(2) Couple on elephant
(3) Standing tīrthaṅkara X
(4) Man with attendants (damaged)
(5) Standing figure X
(6) Standing devotee in *añjali*
(7) Seated tīrthaṅkara
(8) Standing devotee in añjali X
(9) Standing figure X

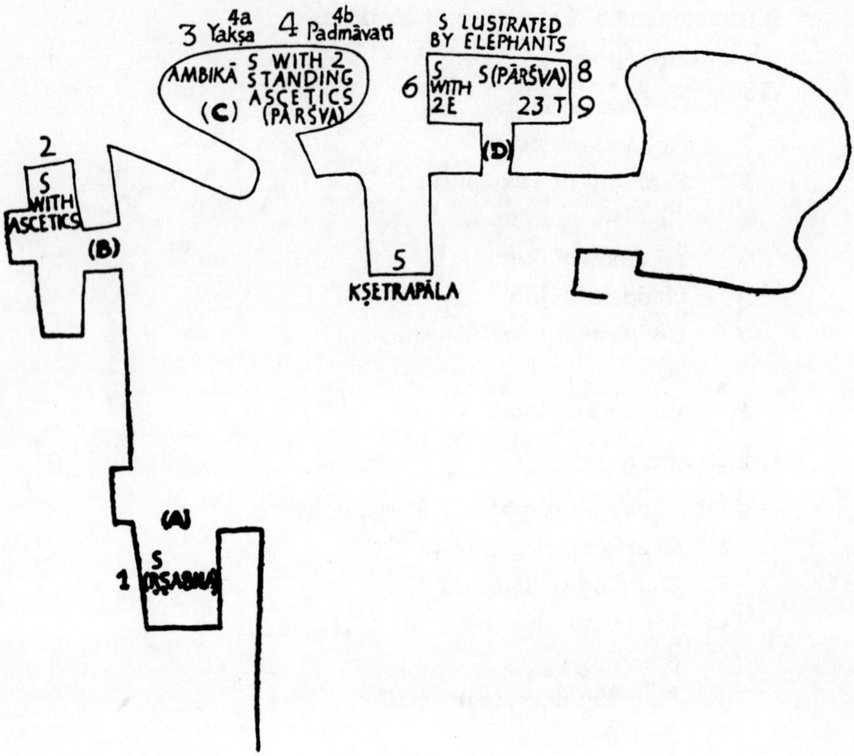
3 Yakṣa
4a
4 Padmāvatī
4b
S LUSTRATED BY ELEPHANTS
AMBIKĀ
S WITH 2 STANDING ASCETICS (PĀRŚVA)
(C)
6
S WITH 2E
S (PĀRŚVA)
23 T
8
9
(D)
2
S WITH ASCETICS
(B)
5
KṢETRAPĀLA
(A)
1
S (ṚṢABHA)

J 5

A 1 Ṛṣabhanātha seated

B 2 Seated tīrthaṅkara with other ascetics (4 visible, others unfinished)

C 3 Ambikā

4 Pārśvanātha seated with two standing ascetics

4a Yakṣa

4b Padmāvatī

5 Kṣetrapāla

D 6 Seated tīrthaṅkara with two standing tīrthaṅkaras

7 Seated tīrthaṅkara lustrated by elephants

8 Pārśvanātha seated

9 23 tīrthaṅkaras

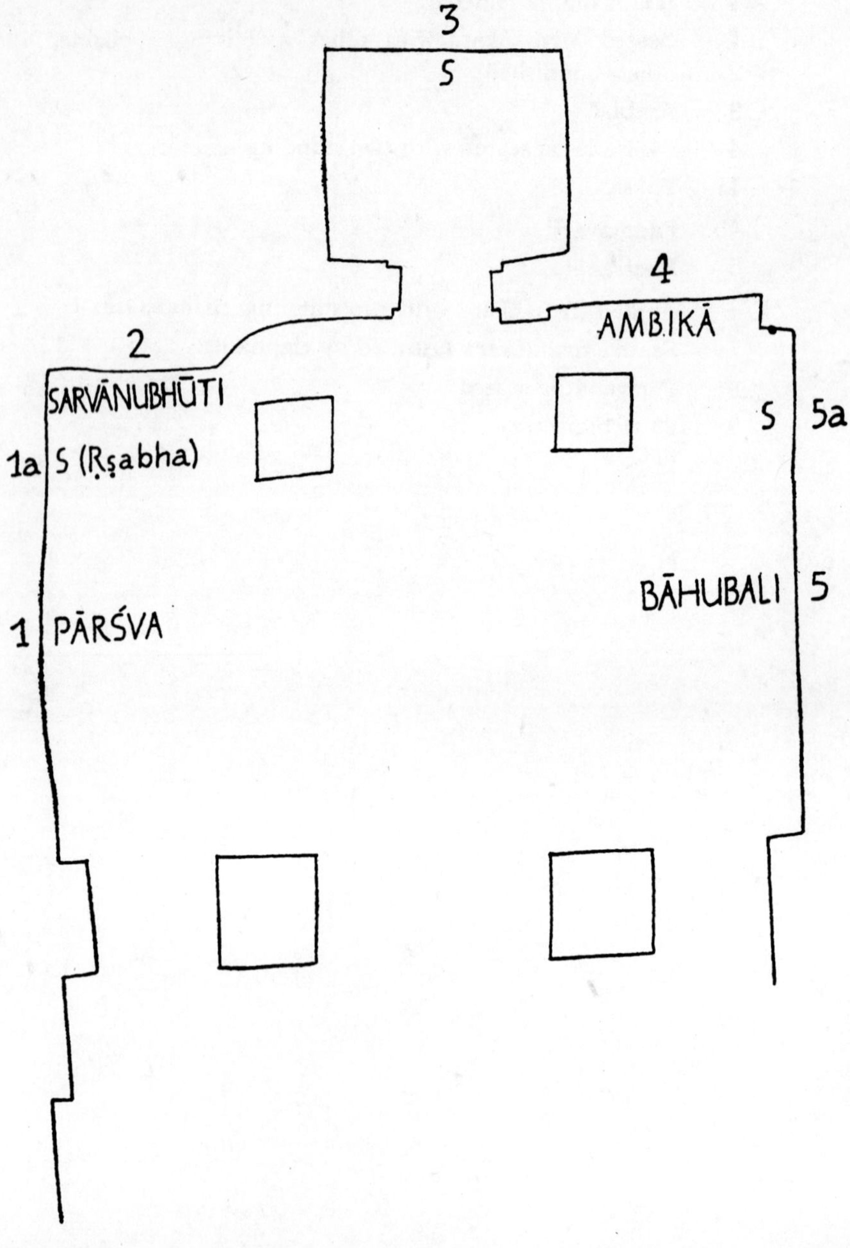
3
S
4
AMBIKĀ
2
SARVĀNUBHŪTI
S
5a
1a
S (Ṛṣabha)
BĀHUBALI
5
1
PĀRŚVA

J 6

1 Pārśvanātha
1a Seated Ṛṣabha
2 Sarvānubhūti
3 Seated tīrthaṅkara
4 Ambikā
5 Bāhubali
5a Seated tīrthaṅkara

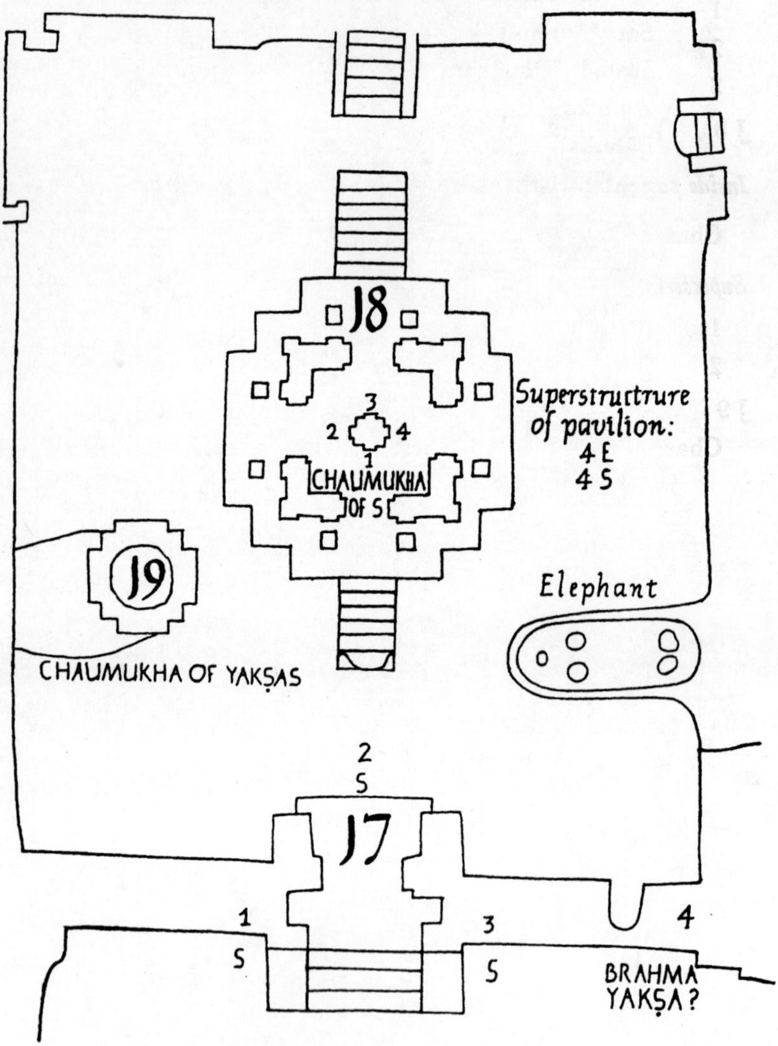
J8
3
2 4
1
CHAUMUKHA OF S
Superstructure of pavilion:
4 E
4 S
J9
CHAUMUKHA OF YAKṢAS
Elephant
2
S
J7
1
S
3
S
4
BRAHMA YAKṢA ?

J 7, J 8, J 9

J 7

1 Seated tīrthaṅkara (left of entrance)

2 Seated tīrthaṅkara (right of entrance)

3 Seated tīrthaṅkara (inside centre of entrance)

J 8 (Pavilion in courtyard)

Inside pavilion

Chaumukha with 4 seated tīrthaṅkaras

Superstructure of pavilion

1 Four panels of a standing tīrthaṅkara each

2 Four panels of a seated tīrthaṅkara each

J 9

Chaumukha of *yakṣas*

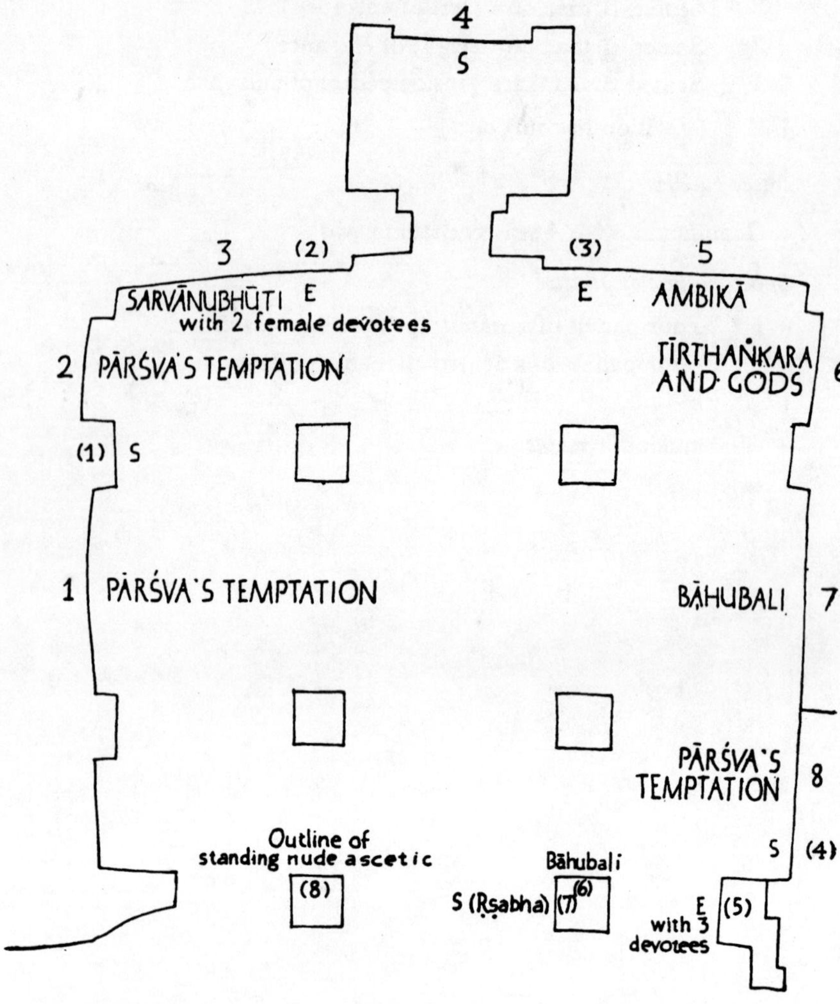
4
S
3
(2)
(3)
5
SARVĀNUBHŪTI
E
with 2 female devotees
E
AMBIKĀ
2
PĀRŚVA'S TEMPTATION
TĪRTHAṄKARA AND GODS
6
(1)
S
1
PĀRŚVA'S TEMPTATION
BĀHUBALI
7
PĀRŚVA'S TEMPTATION
8
Outline of standing nude ascetic
(8)
Bāhubali
(6)
S (Ṛṣabha) (7)
S
(4)
E
with 3 devotees
(5)

J 10

1 Pārśvanātha's temptation
2 Pārśvanātha's temptation
2a Seated tīrthaṅkara (above Pārśvanātha)
3 Sarvānubhūti
4 Seated tīrthaṅkara
5 Ambikā
6 Tīrthaṅkara and gods
7 Bāhubali
8 Pārśvanātha's temptation
(1) Seated tīrthaṅkara
(2) Standing tīrthaṅkara with 2 female devotees
(3) Standing tīrthaṅkara X
(4) Seated tīrthaṅkara
(5) Standing tīrthaṅkara with 3 devotees
(6) Bāhubali
(7) Seated Ṛṣabha
(8) Outline of standing nude ascetic

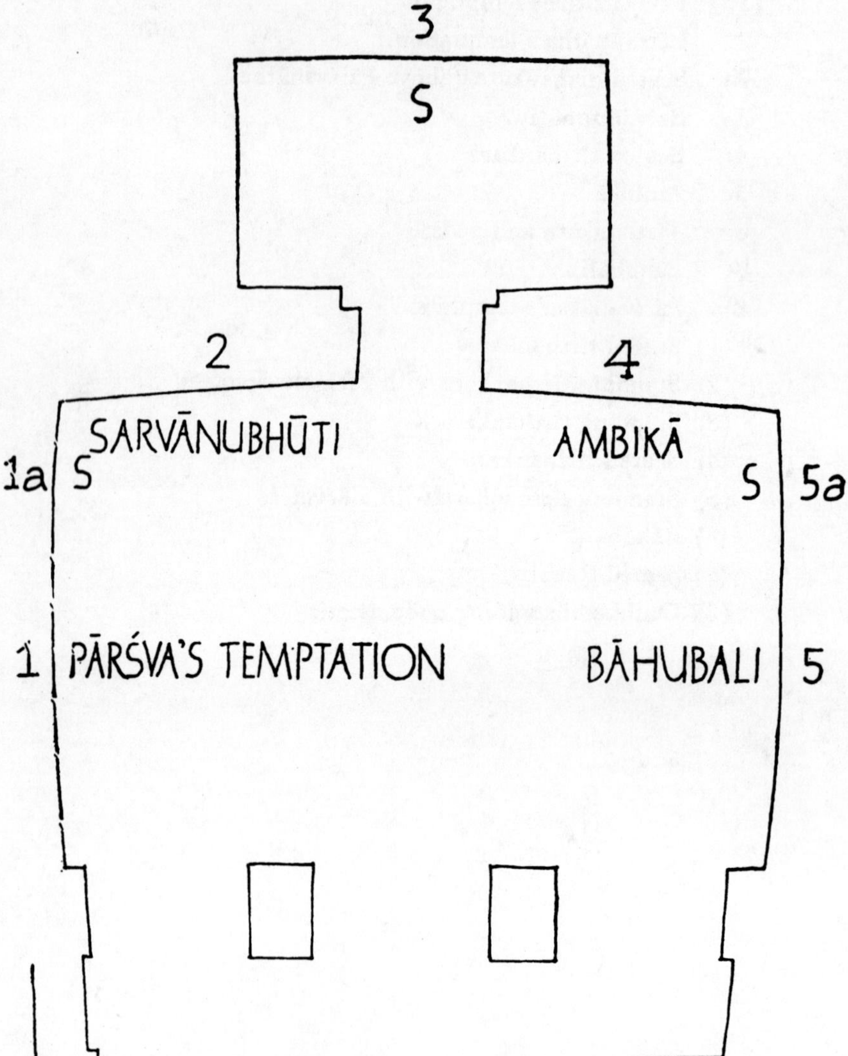
3
S
2
4
SARVĀNUBHŪTI
AMBIKĀ
1a
S
S
5a
1
PĀRŚVA'S TEMPTATION
BĀHUBALI
5

J 11

CLIFF WALL RELIEFS TO LEFT OF J 11

1 Pārśvanātha seated (top)
2 *Sthāpanācārya* and 4 readers (centre)
3 Battle scene (bottom)

INTERIOR

1 Pārśvanātha's temptation
1a Seated tīrthaṅkara
2 Sarvānubhūti
3 Seated tīrthaṅkara
4 Ambikā
5 Bāhubali
5a Seated tīrthaṅkara

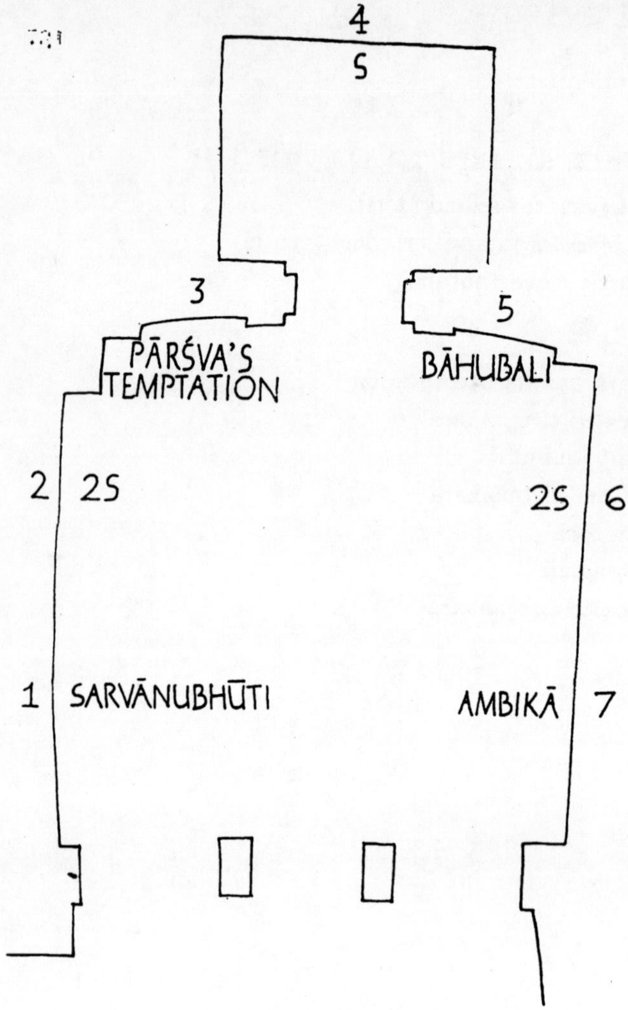
4
S
3
PĀRŚVA'S TEMPTATION
5
BĀHUBALI
2
2S
2S
6
1
SARVĀNUBHŪTI
AMBIKĀ
7

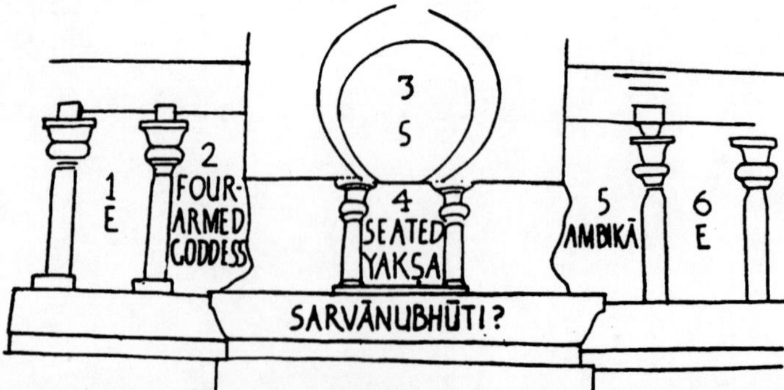
3
S
1
E
2
FOUR-ARMED GODDESS
4
SEATED YAKṢA
5
AMBIKĀ
6
E
SARVĀNUBHŪTI?

Façade

J 12

FACADE

1 Standing tīrthaṅkara
2 4-armed goddess
3 Seated tīrthaṅkara
4 Seated *yakṣa* (Sarvānubhūti ?)
5 Ambikā
6 Standing tīrthaṅkara
7 Gajalakṣmī

INTERIOR

1 Sarvānubhūti
2 Seated tīrthaṅkara
3 Pārśvanātha's temptation
4 Seated tīrthaṅkara
5 Bāhubali
6 Two seated tīrthaṅkaras
7 Ambikā

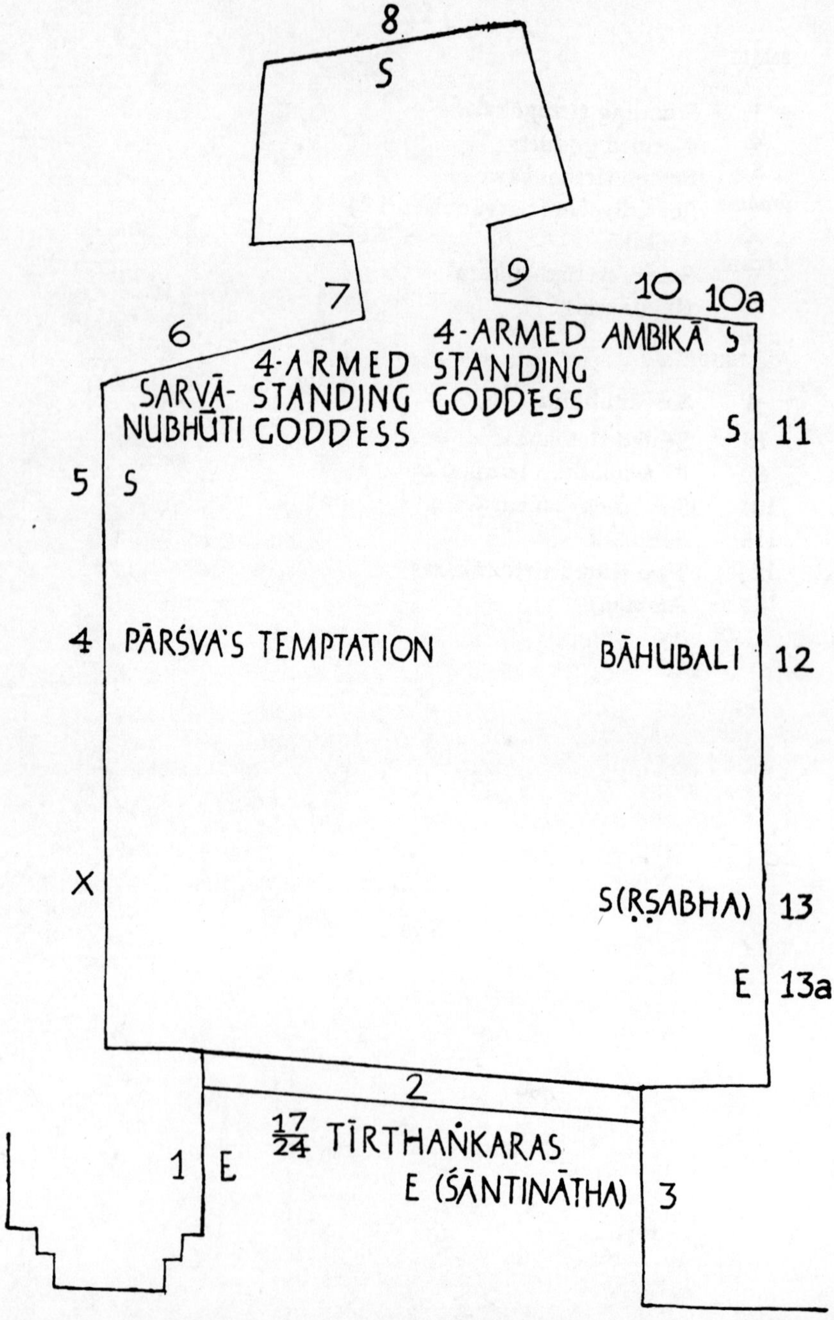
8
S
7
9
10
10a
6
4-ARMED AMBIKĀ
S
4-ARMED STANDING GODDESS
4-ARMED STANDING GODDESS
SARVĀNUBHŪTI
S
11
5
S
4
PĀRŚVA'S TEMPTATION
BĀHUBALI
12
X
S(ṚṢABHA)
13
E
13a
2
17/24 TĪRTHAṄKARAS
1
E
E (ŚĀNTINĀTHA)
3

J 13

SMALL VESTIBULE BEFORE CAVE

1 Standing tīrthaṅkara
2 17/24 tīrthaṅkaras (7 unfinished)
3 Standing tīrthaṅkara (Śāntinātha) with Sohila the *brahmacārin*

INTERIOR OF CAVE

4 Pārśvanātha's temptation
5 Seated tīrthaṅkara
6 Sarvānubhūti
7 4-armed standing goddess
8 Seated tīrthaṅkara
9 4-armed standing goddess
10 Ambikā
11 Seated tīrthaṅkara
12 Bāhubali
13 Seated Ṛṣabha

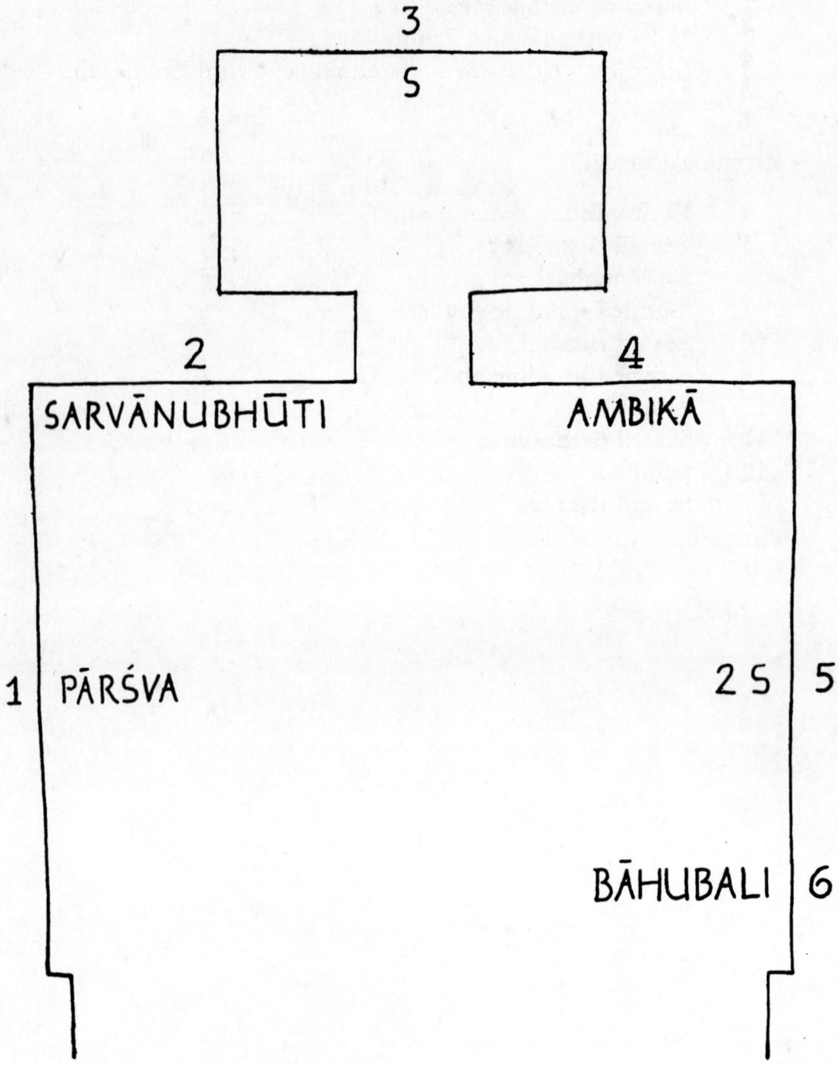
3
5
2
4
SARVĀNUBHŪTI
AMBIKĀ
1
PĀRŚVA
2 5
5
BĀHUBALI
6

J 14

1 Pārśvanātha
2 Sarvānubhūti
3 Seated tīrthaṅkara
4 Ambikā
5 Two seated tīrthaṅkaras
6 Bāhubali

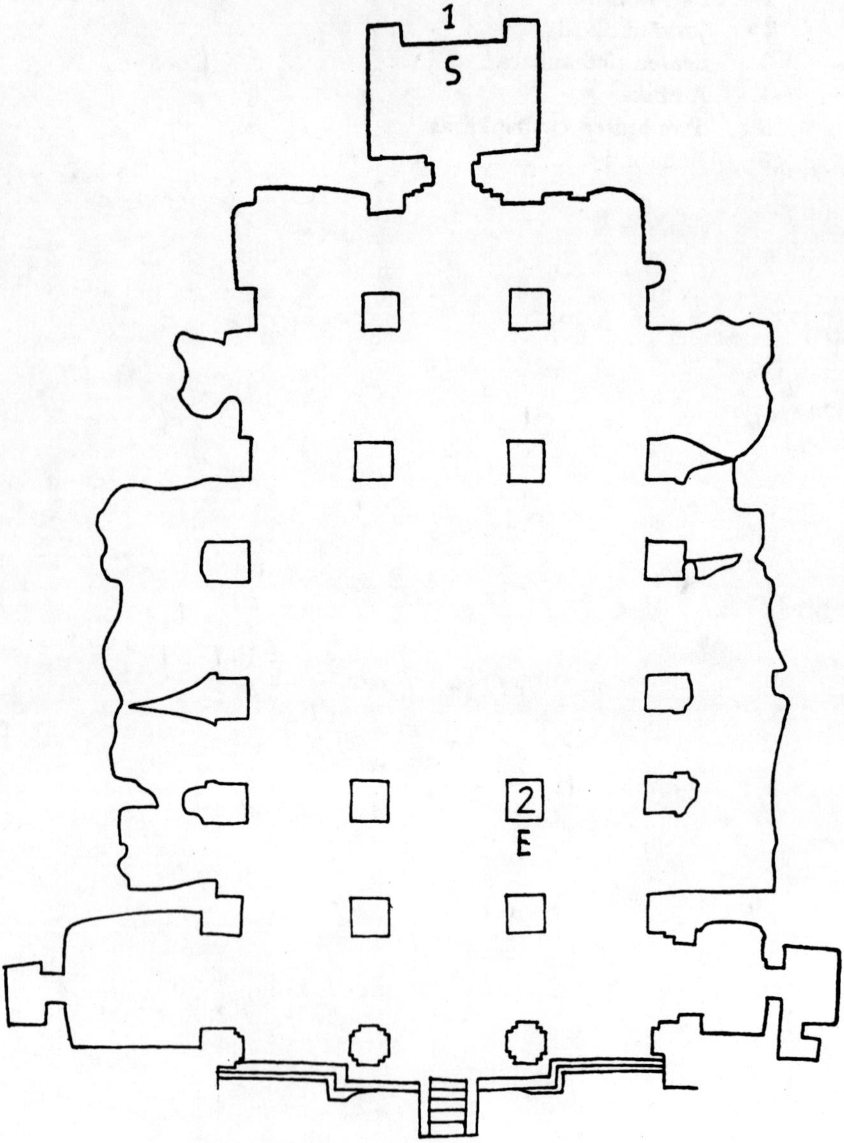
1
S
2
E

J 15

1 Seated tīrthaṅkara
2 Standing tīrthaṅkara

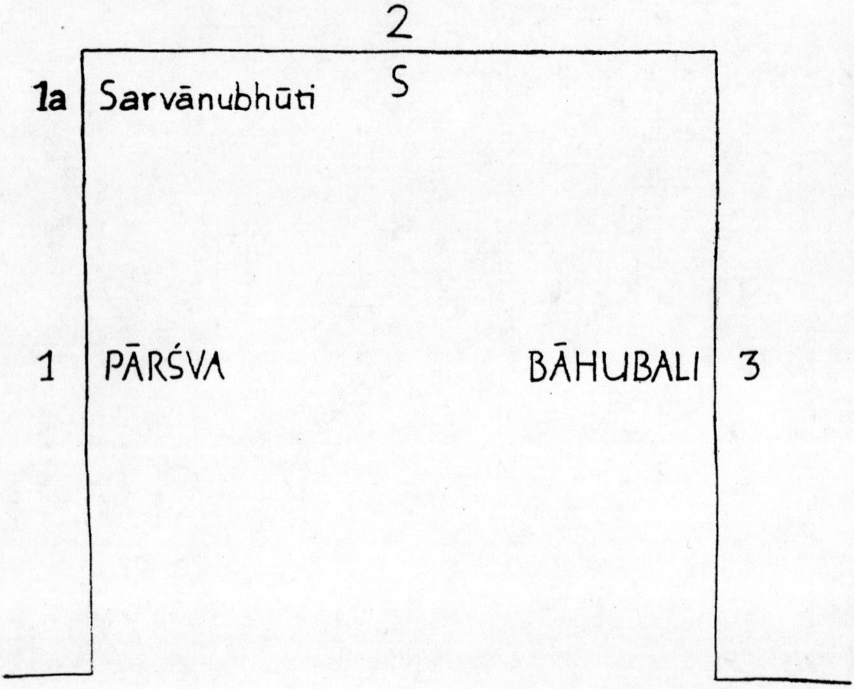
2
S
1a Sarvānubhūti
1 PĀRŚVA
BĀHUBALI 3

J 16

1 Pārśvanātha
1a Sarvānubhūti
2 Seated tīrthaṅkara
3 Bāhubali

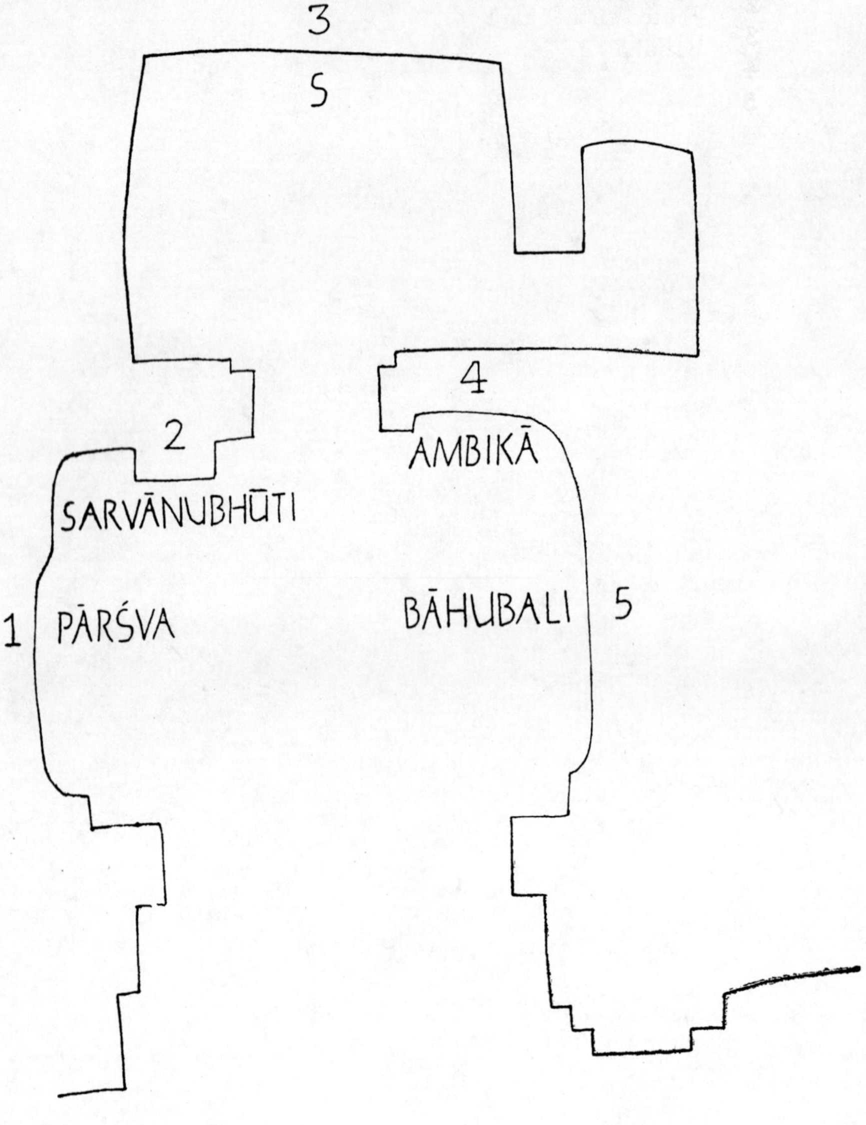
3
5
4
2
AMBIKĀ
SARVĀNUBHŪTI
1
PĀRŚVA
BĀHUBALI
5

J 17

1 Pārśvanātha
2 Sarvānubhūti
3 Seated tīrthaṅkara
4 Ambikā
5 Bāhubali

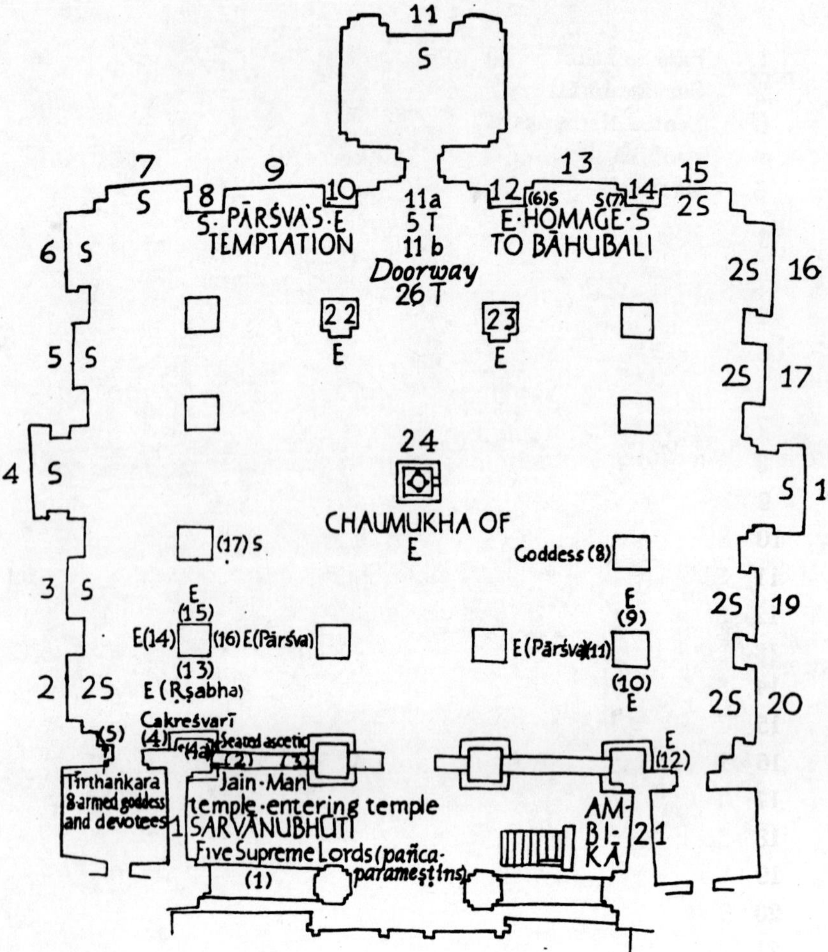

Façade (attic)

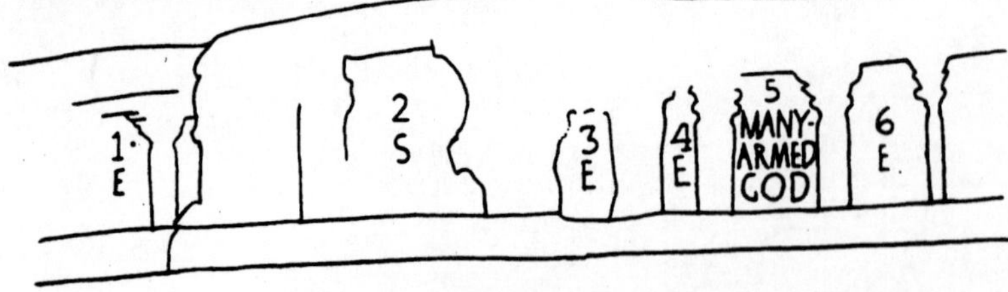

J 18

INTERIOR

1 Sarvānubhūti
2 Seated Ṛṣabha and seated tīrthaṅkara
3 Two seated tīrthaṅkaras
4 Seated tīrthaṅkara
5 Seated tīrthaṅkara
6 (incomplete) Seated tīrthaṅkara
7 Seated tīrthaṅkara
8 Seated tīrthaṅkara
9 Pārśvanātha's temptation
10 Standing tīrthaṅkara
11 Seated tīrthaṅkara
12 Standing tīrthaṅkara
13 Homage to Bāhubali
14 Seated tīrthaṅkara
15 Two seated tīrthaṅkaras
16 Two seated tīrthaṅkaras
17 Two seated tīrthaṅkaras
18 Seated tīrthaṅkara
19 Two seated tīrthaṅkaras
20 Two seated tīrthaṅkaras
21 Ambikā
22 Standing tīrthaṅkara
23 Standing tīrthaṅkara
24 Four standing tīrthaṅkaras X

FACADE

1 Standing tīrthaṅkara
2 Seated tīrthaṅkara
3 Standing tīrthaṅkara
4 Standing tīrthaṅkara
5 Many-armed god
6 Standing tīrthaṅkara

MINOR SCULPTURES

(1) Pañcaparameṣṭins
(2) Man entering temple
(3) Jain temple
(4) Cakreśvarī
(5) Tīrthaṅkara, 4-armed goddess and devotees
(6) Seated tīrthaṅkara
(7) Seated tīrthaṅkara
(8) Goddess on lotus
(9) Standing tīrthaṅkara
(10) Standing tīrthaṅkara
(11) Pārśvanātha standing
(12) 2 standing tīrthaṅkaras
(13) Standing Ṛṣabha
(14) Standing tīrthaṅkara
(15) Standing tīrthaṅkara
(16) Standing Pārśvanātha

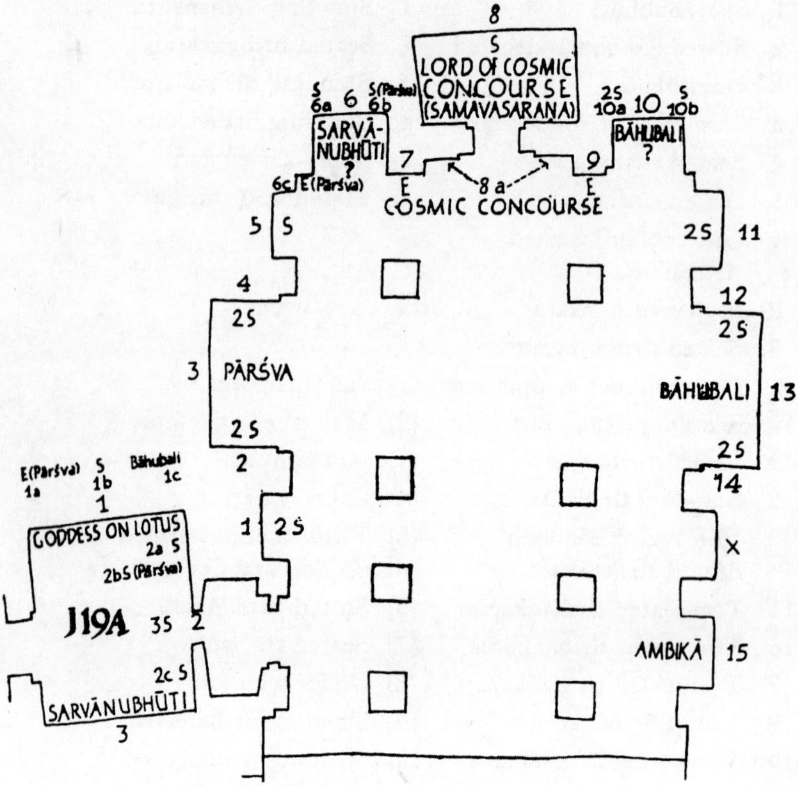
8
S
LORD OF COSMIC CONCOURSE (SAMAVASARANA)
S 6a 6 S(Pārśva) 6b
SARVĀNUBHŪTI ?
7
6c E(Pārśva)
E
8 a
COSMIC CONCOURSE
E
9
2S 10a 10 S 10b
BĀHUBALI ?
5 S
4
2S
3 PĀRŚVA
2S
2
E(Pārśva) 1a
S 1b
Bāhubali 1c
1
GODDESS ON LOTUS
2a S
2bS (Pārśva)
1 2S
J19A
3S 2
2c S
SARVĀNUBHŪTI
3
2S 11
12
2S
BĀHUBALI 13
2S
14
×
AMBIKĀ 15

Façade

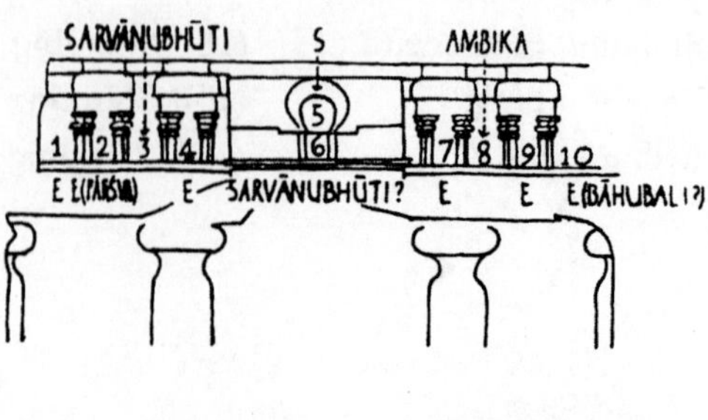
SARVĀNUBHŪTI
S
AMBIKA
1 2 3 4 5 6 7 8 9 10
E E(PĀRŚVA) E SARVĀNUBHŪTI? E E E(BĀHUBALI?)

J 19 and J 19 A

FACADE

1 Standing tīrthaṅkara
2 Standing Pārśvanātha
3 Sarvānubhūti
4 Standing tīrthaṅkara
5 Seated tīrthaṅkara
6 Sarvānubhūti ?
7 Nāga devotee
8 Standing tīrthaṅkara
9 Ambikā
10 Standing tīrthaṅkara
11 Homage to Bāhubali

J 19 A

1 4-armed goddess on lotus (figure X) with three tīrthaṅkaras.
2 Three sitting tīrthaṅkaras, the central one being Pārśvanātha
3 Sarvānubhūti

J 19

1 Two seated tīrthaṅkaras
2 Two seated tīrthaṅkaras
3 Pārśvanātha
4 Two seated tīrthaṅkaras
5 Two seated tīrthaṅkaras
6 Seated tīrthaṅkara
6a Seated tīrthaṅkara
6b Seated Pārśvanātha
6c Standing Pārśvanātha
7 Standing tīrthaṅkara
8 Seated tīrthaṅkara, Lord of the Samavasaraṇa
9 Standing tīrthaṅkara
10 Two seated tīrthaṅkaras
10a Seated Pārśvanātha
10b Seated tīrthaṅkara
11 Two seated tīrthaṅkaras
12 Two seated tīrthaṅkaras
13 Bāhubali
14 Two seated tīrthaṅkaras
15 Ambikā

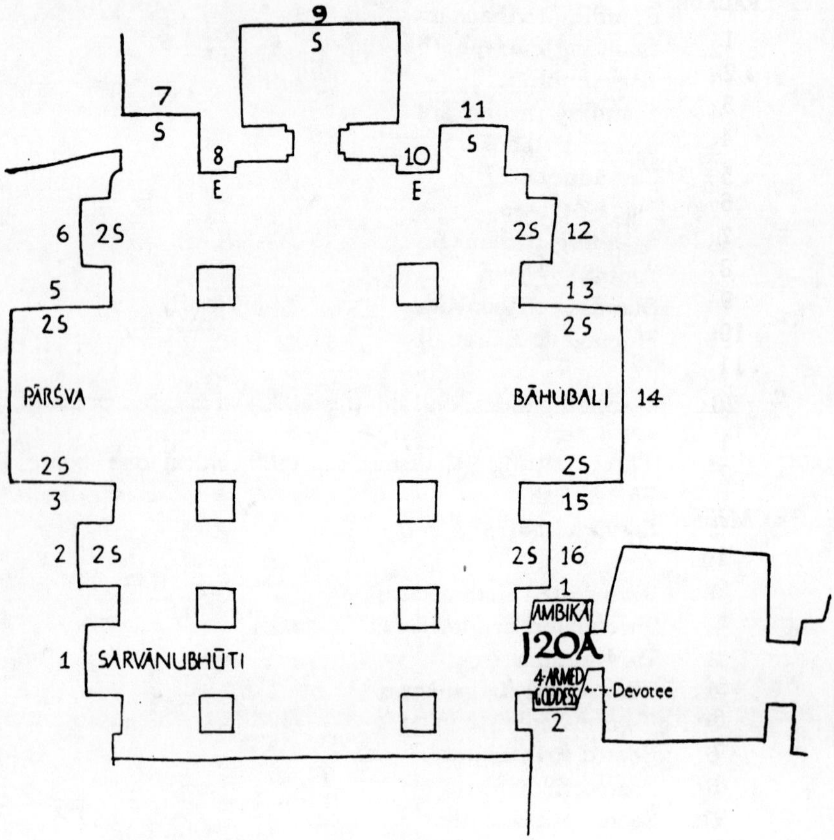
9
S
7
S
8
E
10
E
11
S
6
2S
2S
12
5
13
2S
2S
4
PĀRŚVA
BĀHUBALI
14
2S
2S
3
15
2
2S
2S
16
1
AMBIKĀ
1
SARVĀNUBHŪTI
J20A
4-ARMED GODDESS
Devotee
2

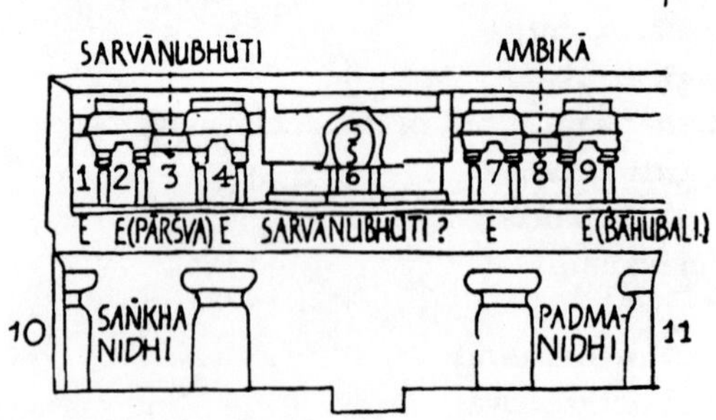
SARVĀNUBHŪTI
AMBIKĀ
1
2
3
4
6
7
8
9
E
E(PĀRŚVA)
E
SARVĀNUBHŪTI ?
E
E(BĀHUBALI)
10
SAṄKHA NIDHI
PADMA NIDHI
11

Façade

J 20 and J 20 A

FACADE

1 Standing tīrthaṅkara
2 Standing Pārśvanātha
3 Sarvānubhūti
4 Standing tīrthaṅkara
5 Seated tīrthaṅkara
6 Yakṣa (Sarvānubhūti?)
7 Standing tīrthaṅkara
8 Ambikā
9 Bāhubali
10 Śaṅkhanidhi
11 Padmanidhi

J 20A

1 Ambikā
2 4-handed goddess

Main sculpture

1 Sarvānubhūti
2 Two seated tīrthaṅkaras
3 Two seated tīrthaṅkaras
4 Pārśvanātha
5 Two seated tīrthaṅkaras
6 Two seated tīrthaṅkaras
7 Seated tīrthaṅkara
8 Standing tīrthaṅkara
9 Seated tīrthaṅkara
10 Standing tīrthaṅkara
11 Seated tīrthaṅkara
12 Two seated tīrthaṅkaras
13 Two seated tīrthaṅkaras
14 Bāhubali
15 Two seated tīrthaṅkaras
16 Two seated tīrthaṅkaras

Minor sculptures

(1) Small seated tīrthaṅkara
(2) Small standing tīrthaṅkara
(3) Small seated tīrthaṅkara

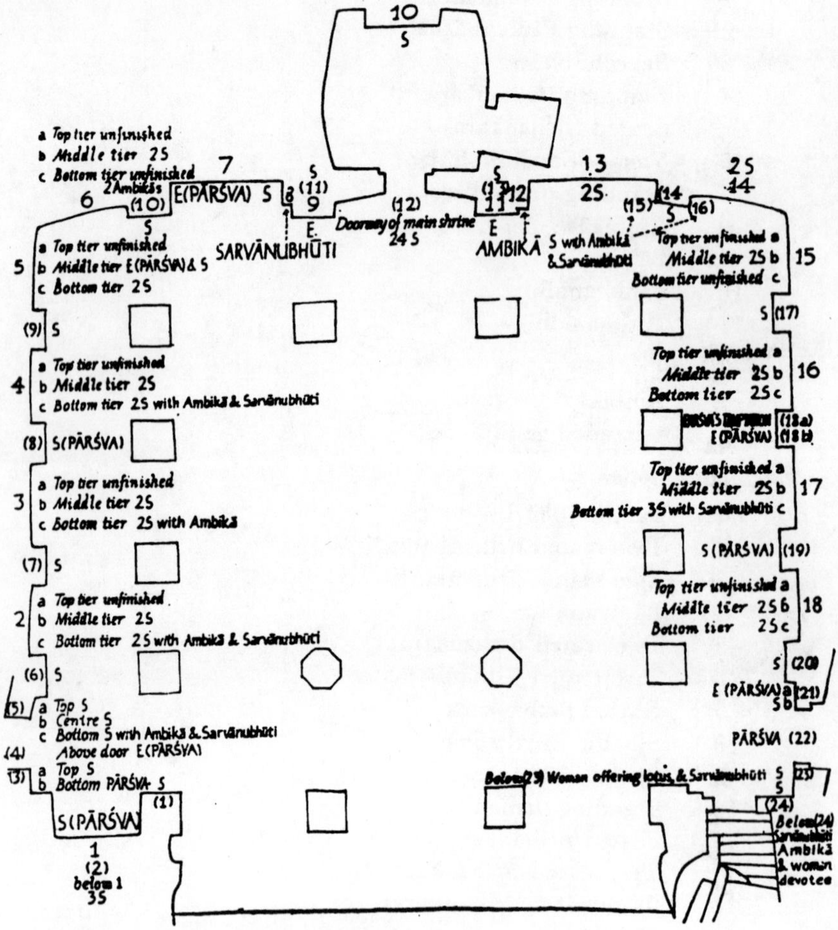
10
S
a Top tier unfinished
b Middle tier 2S
c Bottom tier unfinished
2 Ambikās
6
(10)
S
7
E(PĀRŚVA) S
8
S (11)
9
E.
SARVĀNUBHŪTI
(12)
Doorway of main shrine
24 S
S
(13)
11
12
E
AMBIKĀ
13
2S
S with Ambikā & Sarvānubhūti
(15)
14
S
(16)
2S
14
Top tier unfinished a
Middle tier 2S b
Bottom tier unfinished c
15
a Top tier unfinished
b Middle tier E(PĀRŚVA) & S
c Bottom tier 2S
5
(9) S
S (17)
a Top tier unfinished
b Middle tier 2S
c Bottom tier 2S with Ambikā & Sarvānubhūti
4
Top tier unfinished a
Middle tier 2S b
Bottom tier 2S c
16
(8) S(PĀRŚVA)
E(PĀRŚVA) (18b)
(18a)
a Top tier unfinished
b Middle tier 2S
c Bottom tier 2S with Ambikā
3
Top tier unfinished a
Middle tier 2S b
Bottom tier 3S with Sarvānubhūti c
17
(7) S
S(PĀRŚVA) (19)
a Top tier unfinished
b Middle tier 2S
c Bottom tier 2S with Ambikā & Sarvānubhūti
2
Top tier unfinished a
Middle tier 2S b
Bottom tier 2S c
18
(6) S
S (20)
E (PĀRŚVA) a
S b
(21)
(5) a Top S
b Centre S
c Bottom S with Ambikā & Sarvānubhūti
(4) Above door E(PĀRŚVA)
(3) a Top S
b Bottom PĀRŚVA S
PĀRŚVA (22)
Below (23) Woman offering lotus & Sarvānubhūti S
S
(23)
(24)
(1)
S(PĀRŚVA)
1
(2)
below 1
3S
Below (24)
Sarvānubhūti
Ambikā
& woman
devotee

J 21

1 Seated Pārśvanātha
2a (*Top tier*) unfinished
b (*Middle tier*) Two seated tīrthaṅkaras
c (Bottom tier)
Right panel Seated tīrthaṅkara
Left panel Seated tīrthaṅkara
To right of diptych : Ambikā
To left of diptych : Sarvānubhūti
3a (Top tier) As in 2
b (Middle tier) Two seated tīrthaṅkara
Right panel Seated tīrthaṅkara
Left panel Seated tīrthaṅkara
c (Bottom tier) Band divides right panel from left one. On the band : Ambikā with a child
4a (*Top tier*) As in 2
b (*Middle tier*) Two seated tīrthaṅkaras
c (*Bottom tier*) *Right panel*: Seated tīrthaṅkara (in maṇḍapa)
Left panel : Seated tīrthaṅkara (unfinished)
Band divides panels. On the band : Sarvānubhūti. To right of finished panel : Ambikā with a child.
5a (*Top tier*) Unfinished
b (*Middle tier*) *Left* : Standing Pārśvanātha
Right : Seated tīrthaṅkara
5c (*Bottom tier*) *Right panel* : Seated tīrthaṅkara
Left panel : Seated tīrthaṅkara
Panels divided by band in centre, on which is Sarvānubhūti. To the left of panels : Ambikā with a child
6a (*Top tier*) As in 2
b (*Middle tier*) Two seated tīrthaṅkaras
c (Bottom tier) Unfinished. No Sarvānubhūti.
Two Ambikās, one on each side

7 Right figure : Standing tīrthaṅkara
Left figure : Seated Pārśvanātha
8 Sarvānubhūti
9 Standing tīrthaṅkara
10 Seated tīrthaṅkara
11 Standing tīrthaṅkara
12 Ambikā
13 Two seated tīrthaṅkaras
14 Two seated tīrthaṅkaras
15a (Top tier) Unfinished
b (Middle tier) : Two Seated tīrthaṅkaras
c (Bottom tier) : Unfinished
16a (*Top tier*) : Unfinished ?
b (*Middle tier*) : Two seated tīrthaṅkaras and seated Ṛṣabha and seated tīrthaṅkara
c (Bottom tier) : Two seated tīrthaṅkaras
17a (Top tier) : Unfinished
b (Middle tier) : Two seated tīrthaṅkaras
c (Bottom tier) : Three seated tīrthaṅkaras. Bands separate panels. In band separating second from third tīrthaṅkara : Sarvānubhūti.
18a (Top tier) : Unfinished
b (Middle tier) : Two seated tīrthaṅkaras
c (Bottom tier) : *Right panel.* Seated tīrthaṅkara
Left panel. Seated tīrthaṅkara. Ambikā in central band. Sarvānubhūti in band to the left.
(1) Seated tīrthaṅkara
(2) Below 1. Three seated tīrthaṅkaras
(3) a Top left of door : Seated tīrthaṅkara
b Bottom left of door : Pārśvanātha
(4) Above door : Pārśvanātha
(5) a Top right of door : Seated tīrthaṅkara
b Centre right of door : Seated tīrthaṅkara
c Bottom right of door : Seated tīrthaṅkara with Ambikā and Sarvānubhūti
(6) Seated tīrthaṅkara
(7) Seated tīrthaṅkara
(8) Seated Pārśvanātha

(9) Seated tīrthaṅkara

(10) Seated tīrthaṅkara

(11) Seated tīrthaṅkara

(12) Doorway of main shrine : 24 panels in band around central door : 24 Seated tīrthaṅkaras, one in each panel. Panel to left of left pilaster : each a couple of flying figures. 6 panels to right of right pilaster : each with a couple of flying figures.

(13) Seated tīrthaṅkara

(14) Seated tīrthaṅkara

(15) Below pilaster, left panel : Seated tīrthaṅkara with, Ambikā and Sarvānubhūti Above panel (as on a pedestal) ; snake, owl and frog (?)

(16) Below pilaster, right panel : Seated tīrthaṅkara with Ambikā and Sarvānubhūti

(17) Seated tīrthaṅkara

(18) a (top) Pārśvanātha's temptation
b (bottom) Standing Pārśvanātha

(19) Seated tīrthaṅkara

(20) Seated tīrthaṅkara

(21) a (top) Standing Pārśvanātha
b (bottom) Seated tīrthaṅkara

(22) (*above door*) Pārśvanātha seated

(23) In angle of wall: one on each wall : Seated tīrthaṅkara. Panels below throne. Left panel :
woman offering lotus to man. Right panel: Sarvānubhūti.
Panel below right: tīrthaṅkara : Left panel : Sarvānubhūti. Centre panel : Ambikā with child. Right panel : woman devotee.

(24) Above door : Standing Pārśvanātha.

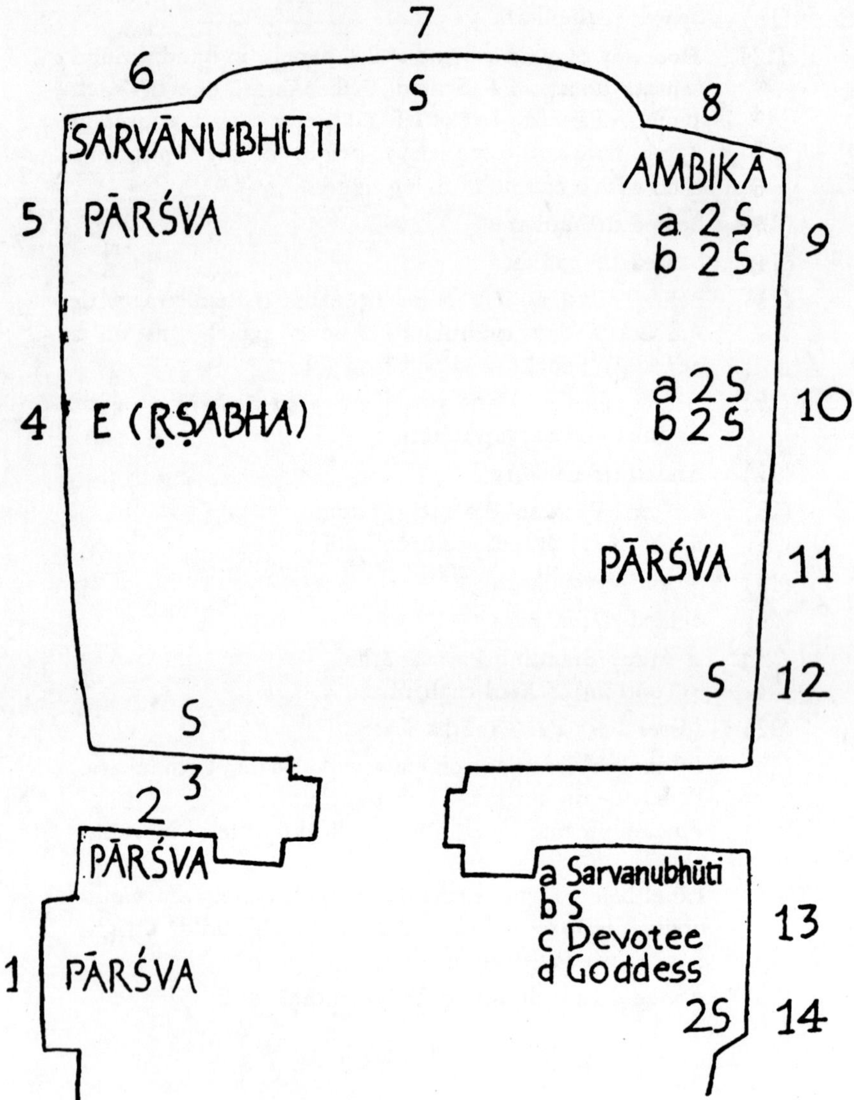
7
6
S
8
SARVĀNUBHŪTI
AMBIKĀ
5
PĀRŚVA
a 2S
b 2S
9
a 2S
b 2S
10
4
E (ṚṢABHA)
PĀRŚVA
11
S
12
S
3
2
PĀRŚVA
a Sarvanubhūti
b S
c Devotee
d Goddess
13
1
PĀRŚVA
2S
14

J 22

1 Pārśvanātha

2 Pārśvanātha

3 Seated tīrthaṅkara (unfinished)

4 Ṛṣabha standing

5 Pārśvanātha

6 Sarvānubhūti

7 Seated tīrthaṅkara

8 Ambikā

9 Tīrthaṅkara panels
a (above) : Two seated tīrthaṅkaras (in 2 panels)
b (below) : Two seated tīrthaṅkaras (in 2 panels)

10 As in 9

11 Pārśvanātha

12 Seated tīrthaṅkara X (only wheel and lions left)

13 Four panels :
a Sarvānubhūti
b Seated tīrthaṅkara
c Devotee in *añjali*
d Goddess

14 Panel fragment : part of two seated tīrthaṅkaras ?

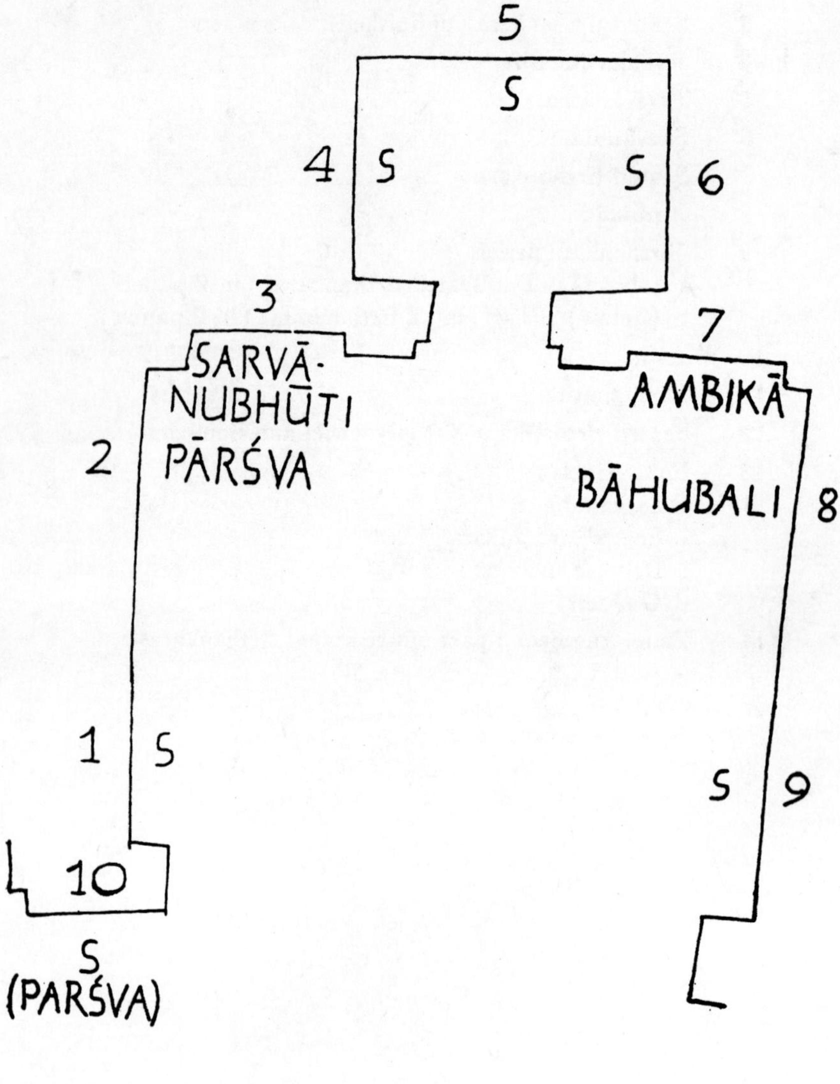
5
S
4
S
S
6
3
7
SARVĀ-
NUBHŪTI
AMBIKĀ
2
PĀRŚVA
BĀHUBALI
8
1
S
S
9
10
S
(PARŚVA)

J 23

1 Seated tīrthaṅkara
2 Pārśvanātha
3 Sarvānubhūti
4 Seated tīrthaṅkara (unfinished)
5 Seated tīrthaṅkara
6 Seated tīrthaṅkara
7 Ambikā
8 Bāhubali
9 Seated tīrthaṅkara
10 Seated Pārśvanātha

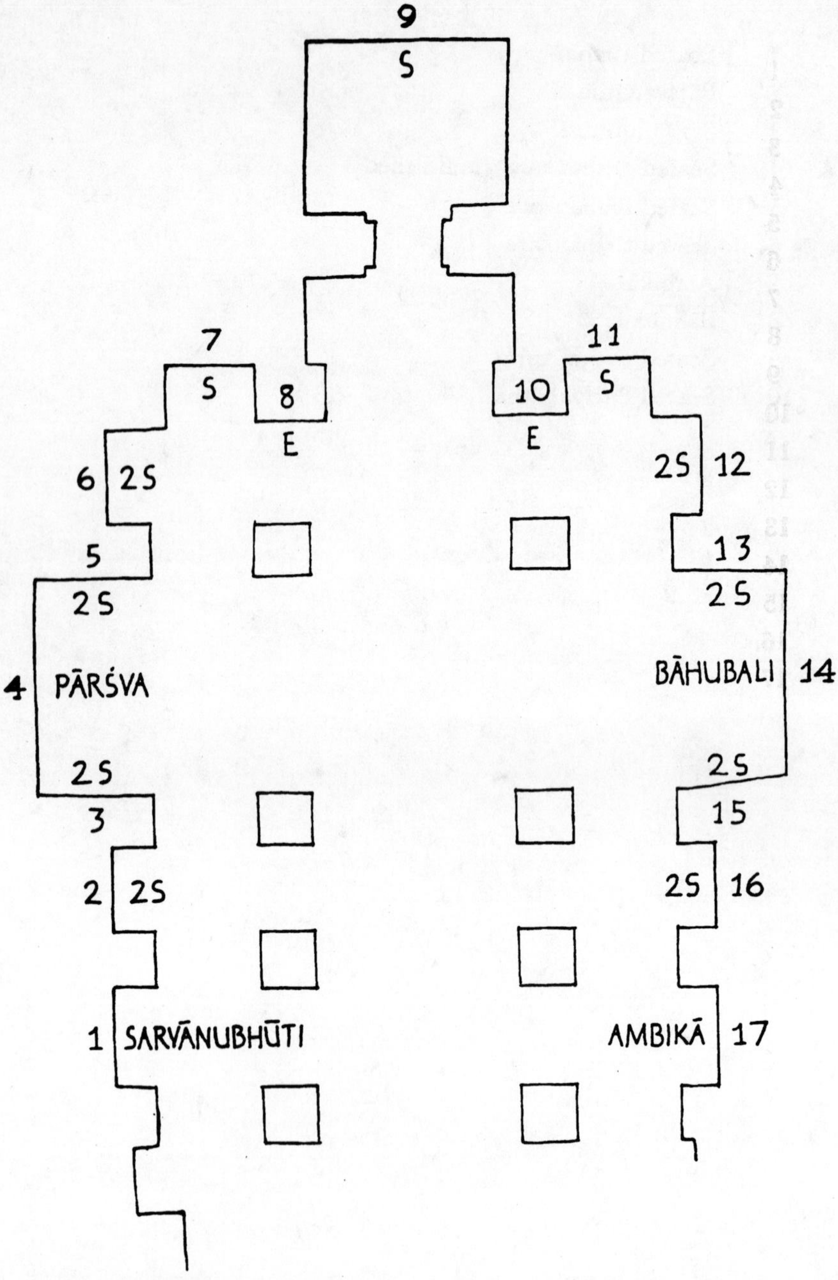
9
S
7
S
8
E
10
E
11
S
6
2S
2S
12
5
13
2S
2S
4
PĀRŚVA
BĀHUBALI
14
2S
2S
3
15
2
2S
2S
16
1
SARVĀNUBHŪTI
AMBIKĀ
17

J 24

1 Sarvānubhūti
2 2 seated tīrthaṅkaras
3 2 seated tīrthaṅkaras
4 Pārśvanātha
5 2 seated tīrthaṅkaras
6 2 seated tīrthaṅkaras
7 Seated tīrthaṅkara
8 Standing tīrthaṅkara
9 Seated tīrthaṅkara (unfinished)
10 Standing tīrthaṅkara
11 Seated tīrthaṅkara
12 2 seated tīrthaṅkaras
13 2 seated tīrthaṅkaras
14 Bāhubali
15 2 seated tīrthaṅkaras
16 2 seated tīrthaṅkaras
17 Ambikā

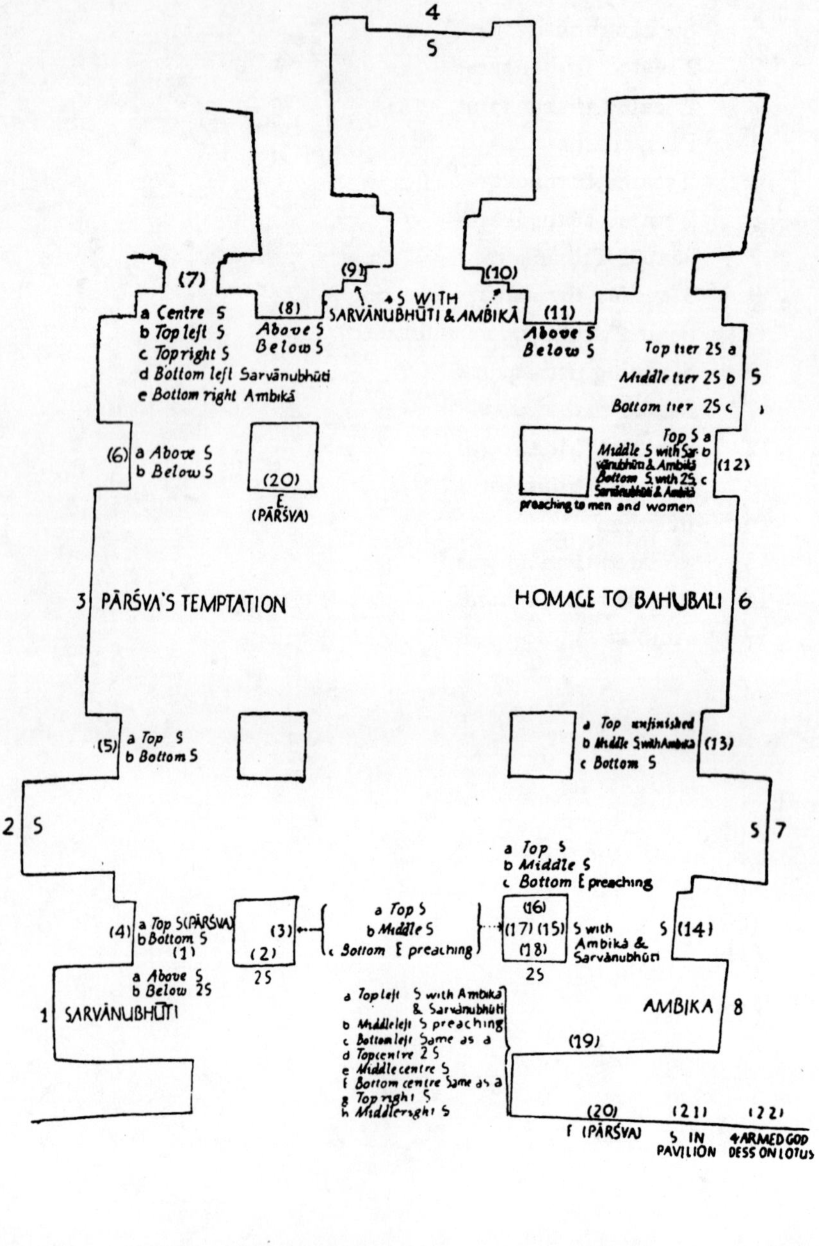
4
S
(7)
a Centre S
b Top left S
c Top right S
d Bottom left Sarvānubhūti
e Bottom right Ambikā
(8)
Above S
Below S
(9)
(10)
4 S WITH SARVĀNUBHŪTI & AMBIKĀ
(11)
Above S
Below S
Top tier 2S a
Middle tier 2S b
Bottom tier 2S c
5
(6) a Above S
b Below S
(20)
E (PĀRŚVA)
Top S a
Middle S with Sarvānubhūti & Ambikā b
Bottom S with 2S, Sarvānubhūti & Ambikā preaching to men and women c
(12)
3 PĀRŚVA'S TEMPTATION
HOMAGE TO BAHUBALI 6
(5) a Top S
b Bottom S
a Top unfinished
b Middle S with Ambikā
c Bottom S
(13)
2 S
S 7
a Top S
b Middle S
c Bottom E preaching
(4) a Top S (PĀRŚVA)
b Bottom S
(1)
(2)
(3)
2S
a Top S
b Middle S
c Bottom E preaching
(16)
(17) (15)
(18)
2S
S with Ambikā & Sarvānubhūti
S (14)
a Above S
b Below 2S
1 SARVĀNUBHŪTI
a Top left S with Ambikā & Sarvānubhūti
b Middle left S preaching
c Bottom left Same as a
d Top centre 2S
e Middle centre S
f Bottom centre Same as a
g Top right S
h Middle right S
AMBIKA 8
(19)
(20)
E (PĀRŚVA)
(21)
S IN PAVILION
(22)
4 ARMED GODDESS ON LOTUS

J 25

1 Sarvānubhūti
2 Seated tīrthaṅkara
3 Pārśvanātha's temptation
4 Seated tīrthaṅkara
5 a (above tier) Two seated tīrthaṅkaras
b (middle tier) Two seated tīrthaṅkaras
c (bottom tier) Two seated tīrthaṅkaras
6 Homage to Bāhubali
7 Seated tīrthaṅkara
8 Ambikā
(1) a (above) Seated tīrthaṅkara
b (below) Two seated tīrthaṅkaras
(2) Two seated tīrthaṅkaras
(3) a (above) Seated tīrthaṅkara
b (middle) Seated tīrthaṅkara
c (bottom) Standing tīrthaṅkara preaching
(4) a (top) Seated Pārśvanātha
b (bottom) Seated tīrthaṅkara
(5) a (top panel) Seated tīrthaṅkara
b (bottom panel) Seated tīrthaṅkara
(6) a (above) Seated tīrthaṅkara
b (below) Seated tīrthaṅkara
(7) a (central panel) Seated tīrthaṅkara
b (top left panel) Seated tīrthaṅkara
c (top right panel) Seated tīrthaṅkara
d (bottom left panel) Sarvānubhūti
e (bottom right panel) Ambikā
(8) a (above) Seated tīrthaṅkara
b (below) Seated tīrthaṅkara
(9) Seated tīrthaṅkara with Sarvānubhūti and Ambikā
(10) Seated tīrthaṅkara with Sarvānubhūti and Ambikā
(11) a (above) Seated tīrthaṅkara
b (below) Seated tīrthaṅkara
(12) a (top) Seated tīrthaṅkara
b (middle) Seated tīrthaṅkara with Sarvānubhūti and Ambikā
c (bottom) Seated tīrthaṅkara (with two seated tīrthaṅkaras Sarvānubhūti, and Ambikā) preaching to men and women.

(13) a (*top panel*) unfinished
b (middle panel) Seated tīrthaṅkara with Ambikā
b (bottom panel) Seated tīrthaṅkara
(14) Seated tīrthaṅkara
(15) Seated tīrthaṅkara with Ambikā and Sarvānubhūti
(16) a (above) Seated tīrthaṅkara
b (middle) Seated tīrthaṅkara
c (bottom) Standing tīrthaṅkara
(17) a (above) Seated tīrthaṅkara
b (middle) Seated tīrthaṅkara
c (bottom) Standing tīrthaṅkara preaching
(18) Two seated tīrthaṅkaras
(19) a (left, top) Seated tīrthaṅkara with Ambikā and Sarvānubhūti
b (left, middle) Standing tīrthaṅkara preaching
c (left, bottom) Seated tīrthaṅkara with Ambikā and Sarvānubhūti
d (centre, top) Two seated tīrthaṅkaras
e (centre, middle) Seated tīrthaṅkara
f (centre, bottom) Seated tīrthaṅkara with Ambikā and Sarvānubhūti
g (right, top) Seated tīrthaṅkara
h (right, middle) Seated tīrthaṅkara
(20) Standing Pārśvanātha
(21) Tīrthaṅkara seated in pavilion
(22) 4-armed goddess on lotus

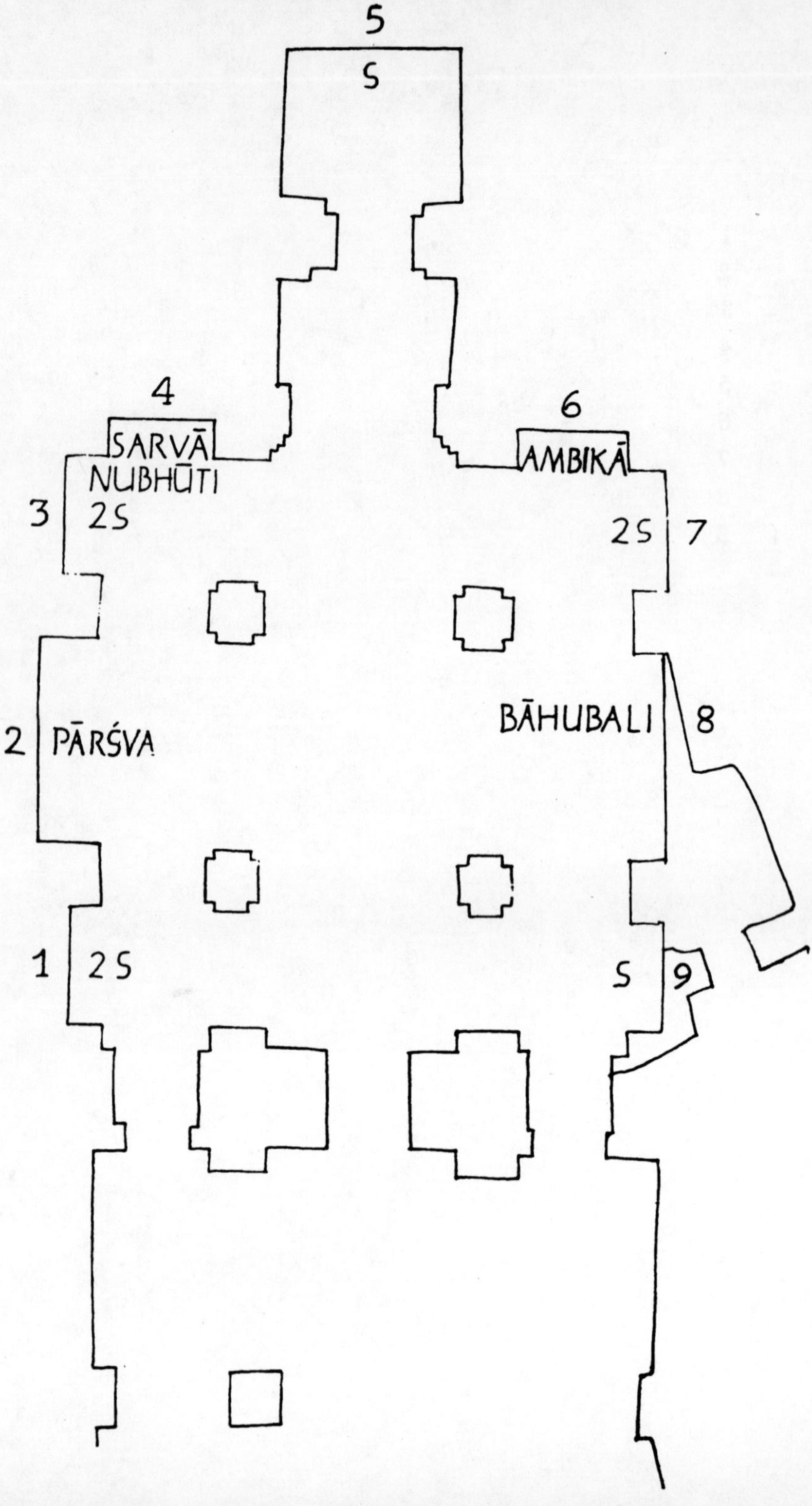
5
S
4
SARVĀ
NUBHŪTI
6
AMBIKĀ
3
2S
2S
7
2
PĀRŚVA
BĀHUBALI
8
1
2S
S
9

J 26

1 Two seated tīrthaṅkaras
2 Pārśvanātha
3 Two seated tīrthaṅkaras
4 Sarvānubhūti
5 Seated tīrthaṅkara
6 Ambikā
7 Two seated tīrthaṅkaras
8 Bāhubali
9 Seated tīrthaṅkara

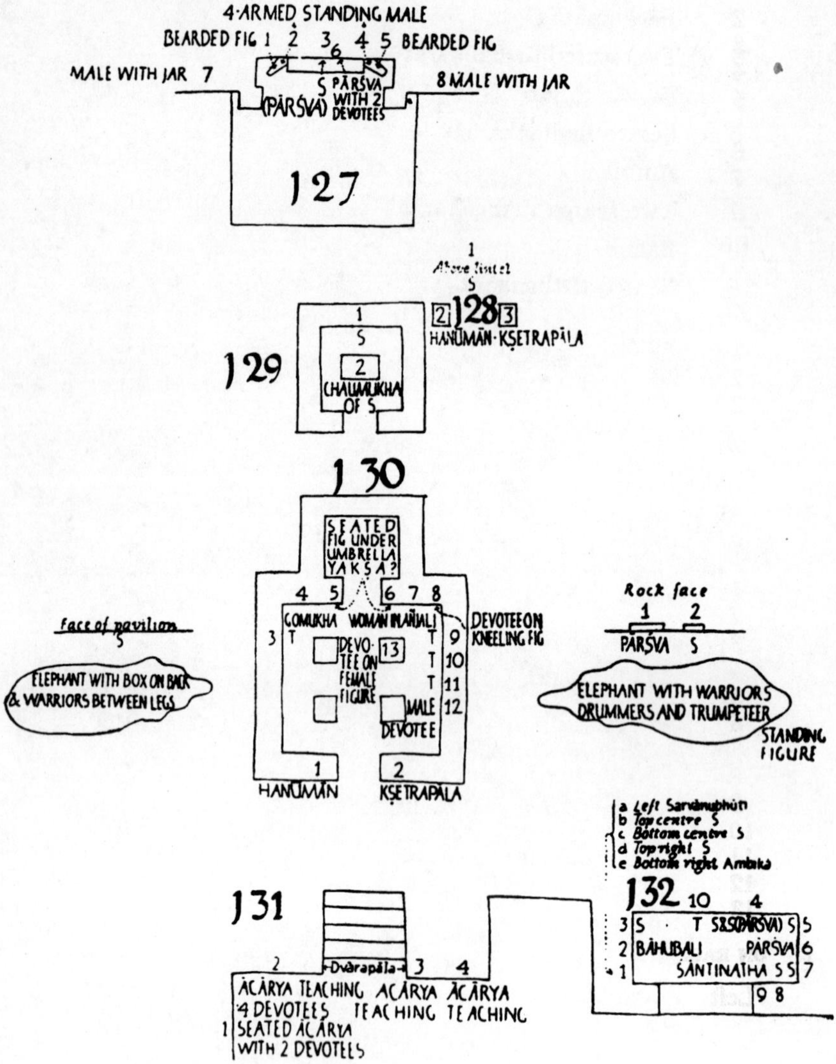
4-ARMED STANDING MALE
BEARDED FIG 1 2 3 6 4 5 BEARDED FIG
MALE WITH JAR 7
8 MALE WITH JAR
S (PĀRŚVA)
PĀRŚVA WITH 2 DEVOTEES
J 127
1
Above lintel
S
2 J128 3
HANUMĀN · KṢETRAPĀLA
J 29
1
S
2
CHAUMUKHA OF S
J 30
SEATED FIG UNDER UMBRELLA YAKṢA?
4 5 6 7 8
GOMUKHA
WOMAN IN AÑJALI
DEVOTEE ON KNEELING FIG
3 T
T 9
T 10
T 11
12
DEVOTEE ON FEMALE FIGURE
13
MALE DEVOTEE
1 HANUMĀN
2 KṢETRAPĀLA
Face of pavilion
S
ELEPHANT WITH BOX ON BACK & WARRIORS BETWEEN LEGS
Rock face
1 2
PĀRŚVA S
ELEPHANT WITH WARRIORS DRUMMERS AND TRUMPETEER
STANDING FIGURE
a Left Sarvānubhūti
b Top centre S
c Bottom centre S
d Top right S
e Bottom right Ambikā
J 31
2 +Dvārapāla+ 3 4
ĀCĀRYA TEACHING 4 DEVOTEES
ĀCĀRYA TEACHING
ĀCĀRYA TEACHING
1 SEATED ĀCĀRYA WITH 2 DEVOTEES
J32 10 4
3 S T S&S(PĀRŚVA) S 5
2 BĀHUBALI PĀRŚVA 6
1 ŚĀNTINĀTHA S S 7
9 8

J 27

1 Bearded figure, cross-legged, with rosary-like wheel between joined hands
2 4-armed standing male
3 Pārśvanātha seated
4 4-armed standing female
5 Bearded figure, cross-legged, with rosary-like wheel between joined hands
6 Small Pārśvanātha, seated with two devotees
7 Large male with jar
8 Large male with jar

J 28, J 29, J 30

J 28

1 Seated tīrthaṅkara
2 Hanumān
3 Kṣetrapāla

J 29

1 Seated tīrthaṅkara X
2 Chaumukha with 4 seated tīrthaṅkaras

J 30

1 Hanumān
2 Kṣetrapāla
3 Tīrthaṅkāra
4 Gomukha *yakṣa*
5 Seated figure under umbrella—*yakṣa* ?
6 Seated figure under umbrella—*yakṣa* ?
7 Woman devotee in *anjali*
8 Devotee held up by kneeling figure
9 Tīrthaṅkara X
10 Tīrthaṅkara X
11 Tīrthaṅkara X
12 Male devotee
13 Devotee borne on female flying figure

ON EACH SIDE OF THE TEMPLE, OUTSIDE

Left Elephant with box on its back and warriors between its legs
1 Seated tīrthaṅkara on face of pavilion opposite it

Right Elephant with warriors, drummers and trumpetteer.
1 Pārśvanātha, (2) seated tīrthaṅkara on panels on rock wall to the animals' right
1 Standing figure behind elephant

J 31 and J 32

J 31

1 Seated *ācārya* (*upādhyāya*) with two devotees
2 *Ācārya* (*upādhyāya*) teaching 4 devotees
3 *Ācārya* (*upādhyāya*) teaching (no devotees)
4 *Ācārya* (*upādhyāya*) teaching

J 32

1a Sarvānubhūti
b Seated tīrthaṅkara
c Seated tīrthaṅkara
d Seated tīrthaṅkara
e Ambikā
2 Bāhubali
3 Seated tīrthaṅkara (with two tīrthaṅkaras at the top corners)
4 Seated tīrthaṅkara (with two seated tīrthaṅkaras and two standing tīrthaṅkaras)
4a Seated Pārśvanātha
5 Seated tīrthaṅkara (with two seated tīrthaṅkaras)
6 Pārśvanātha
7 Seated tīrthaṅkara (with two seated tīrthaṅkaras)
8 Seated tīrthaṅkara
9 Śāntinātha
10 Tīrthaṅkara X on throne with wheel and lions.

Figure 1.
J 31-2. Upādhyāya expounding scriptures.

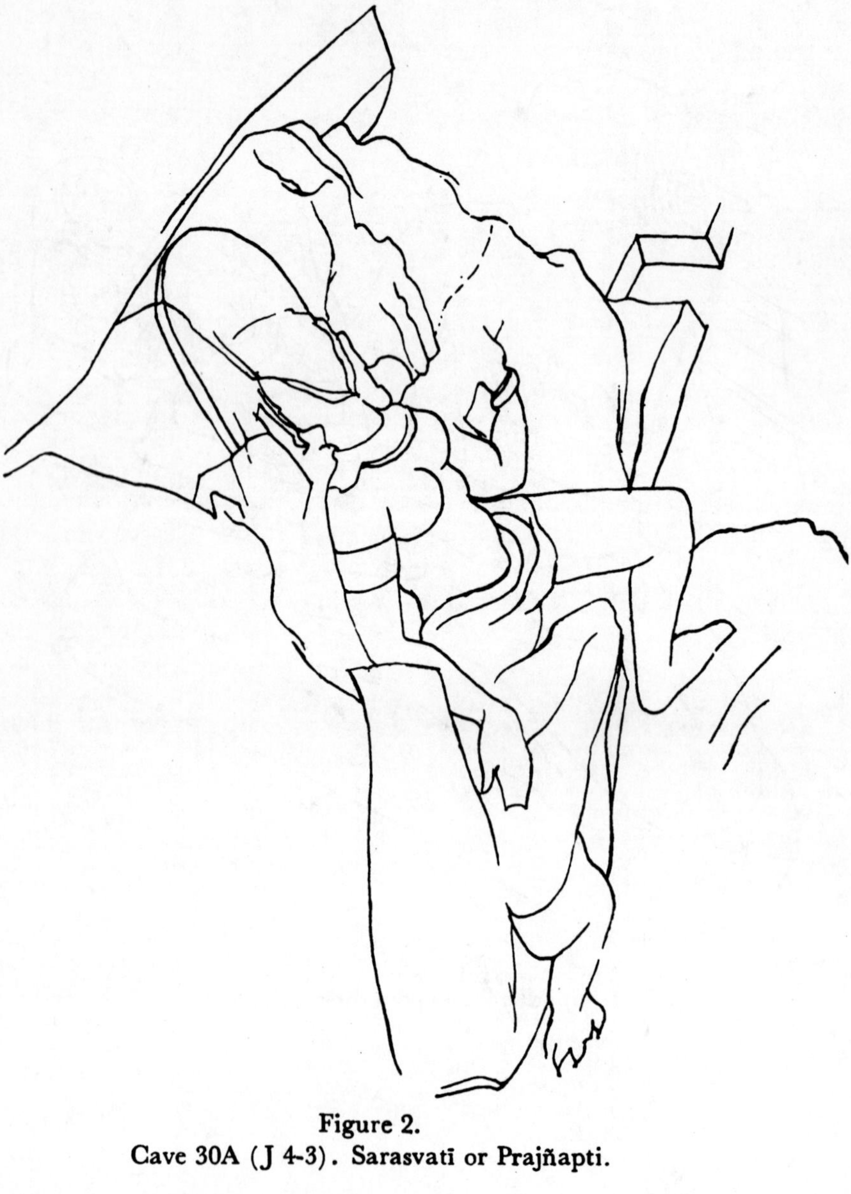

Figure 2.
Cave 30A (J 4-3). Sarasvatī or Prajñapti.

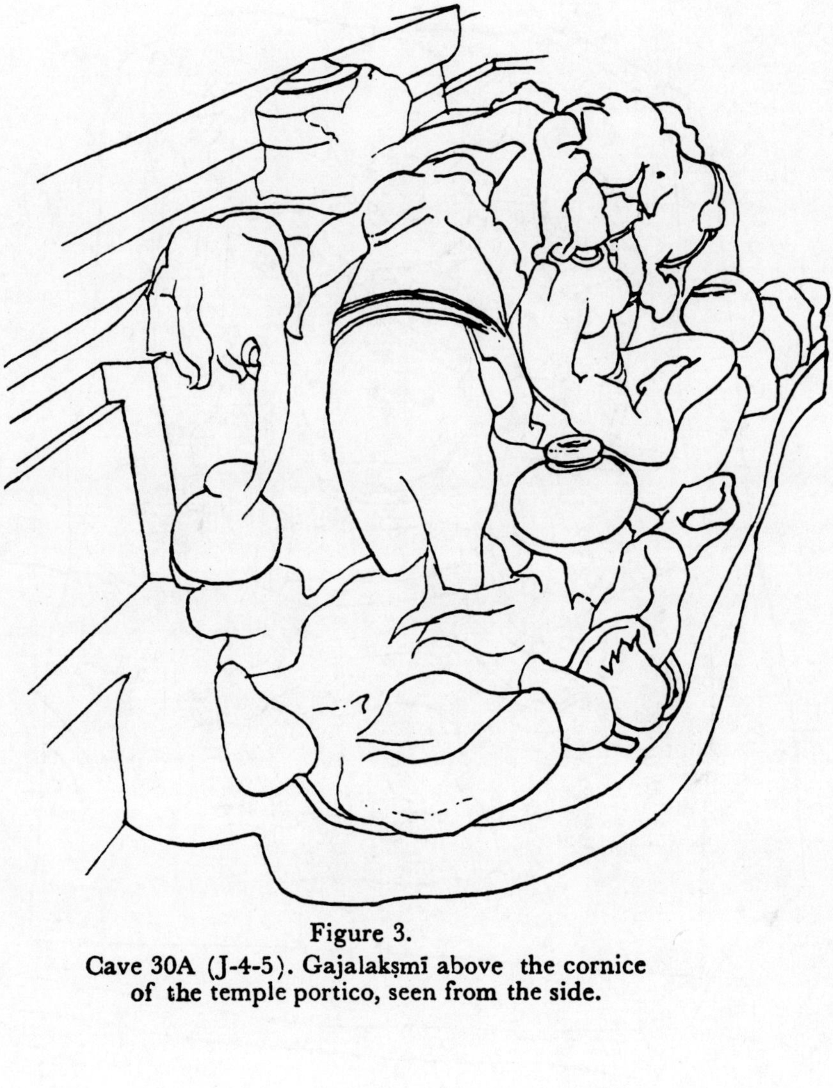

Figure 3.
Cave 30A (J-4-5). Gajalakṣmī above the cornice of the temple portico, seen from the side.

Figure 4.
J 30-4. Gomukha.

Figure 5.
J 5-5. Kṣetrapāla.

Figure 6.
J 31-13. Devout layman.

INDEX

V

Y

Z